FABULOUS

Parties

'Classy, elegant, beautiful... Mark's Garden'

Whoopi Goldberg

FABULOUS *Parties*

FOOD AND FLOWERS FOR ELEGANT ENTERTAINING

MARK HELD, RICHARD DAVID & PEGGY DARK

RYLAND
PETERS
& SMALL

LONDON NEW YORK

Designer **Pamela Daniels**
Senior commissioning editor **Julia Charles**
Location research **Peggy Dark, Mark Held, and Richard David**
Picture manager **Emily Westlake**
Production manager **Patricia Harrington**
Art director **Leslie Harrington**
Publishing director **Alison Starling**

Food stylists **Valerie Aikman-Smith and Robyn Valerik**
Mixologist **Brent Sherman**
Recipe writer **Megan Slaughter**

First published in hardback in the United States in 2008

This paperback edition published in 2010
by Ryland Peters & Small, Inc.
519 Broadway, 5th Floor
New York, NY 10012
www.rylandpeters.com

10 9 8 7 6 5 4 3 2 1

ISBN 978 1 84597 954 6

The hardback edition is catalogued as follows:

Library of Congress Cataloging-in-Publication Data
Held, Mark
  Fabulous parties food and flowers for elegant entertaining / Mark Held, Richard
David, Peggy Dark.
        p. cm.
  Includes index.
  ISBN 978-1-84597-628-6
  1. Entertaining. 2. Cookery. 3. Parties. I. David, Richard. II. Dark, Peggy. III.
Title.
  TX731.H3575 2008
  642'.4--dc22
                                    2007048582

Printed and bound in China

Contents

Introduction

As the famous American hostess Elsa Maxwell said about entertaining in the mid-twentienth century: "Serve the dinner backward, do anything—but for goodness sake, do something weird." It is still a good point. Attempt something new each time your entertain.

"Mark's Garden is like taking a peek into the Gardens of Babylon or, to go back a bit further, the Garden of Eden. I don't know where the flowers come from, but they have an unearthly quality. They are so crisp and alive and the colors are otherworldly. I wish I had their greenhouse, but thankfully they share it with me every season of the year. Whenever friends send me flowers from this haven of beauty I feel like I know what heaven must be like."

Dame Elizabeth Taylor

opposite page
Richard and Mark at work.

Fresh Ideas for Entertaining

Los Angeles is not like other towns. In so many ways. For better or worse. Arguably, its cultural diversity is unsurpassed anywhere else in the world. Geographically, the terrain we call Los Angeles spans from the mountain foothills of Pasadena to the densely populated downtown, across The Valley, the canyons of Hollywood, and Beverly Hills down to the famous beaches of Santa Monica and Malibu. The climate is one of the most pleasant in the world. Except for a few annoyances like traffic congestion, a little smog, and occasional earthquakes, we are very privileged.

Los Angeles has always been The Edge. It has always personified the pioneer spirit, searching for the new, breaking conventions and barriers. To its detriment at times, the old in Los Angeles has always taken backseat to the new. It's always about what's hot and what's the next big thing.

From the earliest beginnings everything here was newly invented. After all, this was basically a desert. The invention has had a lot to do with the original film industry that was built here. Los Angeles was a desolate town with no place to go, nothing to do. Those old time producers, directors, and movie stars not only invented motion pictures, they invented their own entertainment and their own way of living. It became a style that fascinated and influenced people and became emulated around the world. That public enthrallment has continued to this day making Los Angeles a permanent epicenter for entertainment and new trends of all kinds.

As they did from the very beginning people still flock to Los Angeles looking for their new world, new horizons, new adventures, new opportunities, new starts. A huge number of them have made good lives here. Los Angeles is home to some of the most successful, wealthiest, famous, most sophisticated people in the world. Many of these people are our clients and we love them. They give us the opportunity to create fabulous parties for them on a regular basis. It is a challenge to exercise our talents and push beyond normal limits to generate new concepts and styles. Few other places can offer this. Fortunately we have thrived on it. We have tried to give you a little taste of that in this book. We do not intend it to be an instructional guide but we are passing along a few secrets for giving a spectacular party and offer you some inspiration. "Try something new" is our motto and we encourage you to experiment with different ideas each time you entertain. The parties in this book are all based on a theme. It's not mandatory to have a defined theme although that can be fun, but it is best to at least have a point of view in your mind. It's one of the easiest ways to start planning. It encourages you to focus on a look or a feel that can assist you in making

other selections. A sample starting point is to choose a type of food you want to serve or a motif or even just a color. You might have a guest of honor who loves spicy food or the color pink. Maybe someone loves gardening or golf. These are good beginnings to help you plan.

One of the most critical elements of your event is, of course, the food. It must taste good and there must be plenty of it. Even if you are not preparing the quantities we produce at our parties, it helps to approach it the same way we do. If you are doing the cooking, limit the number of ingredients necessary and prepare as much as you can in advance, leaving finishing touches to a minimum.

As your guests gather, the momentum should begin immediately, and that is why we always allow a generous—but not overly extended—cocktail and hors d'oeuvres hour. Cocktails are back in a big way. We always try to create something unusual that fits into the theme of the affair and prepares the palate for the array of food that will follow. Hors d'oeuvres are something you can approach bravely with no-holds-barred. Tidbits of adventurous samplings not only whet the appetite before a meal, they offer entertainment to the palate so nobody makes a great commitment to a

full portion of something. Most guests will try anything new in this way when they wouldn't imagine ordering it for a meal on a night out. Consequently this is really the time to try to give them something new and unexpected—our constant pursuit.

The food and the way it is presented expresses a lot about you, the host, and your regard for those you have gathered around you. A sumptuous feast is often the order of the night, especially for a holiday when most of us want to abandon our restricted diets and celebrate. Damn the waistline! Other events, however, call for a more subdued menu, such as the glorious salad bar we serve for our Pink Luncheon. It may be a light healthy meal, but there is such abundance to the choices that those of us who wish to indulge certainly get the opportunity to eat sumptuously.

Then there is dessert. What can we say about everybody's favorite food group? There is nothing we like better than seeing eyes light up when the desserts are brought out. For most of us they are so hard to resist and it is such a fun part of the affair that we will indulge ourselves, even if we share or just take a tidbit. Or two. We think it is important to always prepare desserts that look as good as they taste because half of the fun is looking. We feel that desserts are so important we created a party around our favorites!

Now the experienced host knows that food shares the stage with flowers at a successful party. Flowers set the mood as they lend an air of fun, sophistication, and festivity. The presence of flowers tells your guests that they are special and that you have gone to great effort to make them feel so. Flowers also help to establish the theme of your party since they can be so expressive in the way they are presented. They are an extension of the enjoyment of the food giving visual pleasure along with the sweet and savory tastes of your menu.

Never underestimate the effect of flowers generally. After all of these years in the business, we are still surprised sometimes at the power flowers can have over people. Like one of our friends who hosts dozens of parties large and small every year has said, "Whenever I send your flowers to people, they like me better." And then she usually adds "You're amazing!" What she really means is that flowers are amazing. She, like most experienced hostesses, would not think of entertaining without flowers surrounding her and her guests. The concept works. Flowers can transform people. They set the scene of a party like nothing else can.

Combined with a careful selection of details like invitations, table settings, and lighting you can establish a mood that captures your guests' imaginations and lends your party a life of its own. It's also important to remember that no party is perfect. There are always a few small glitches. Don't worry if something goes wrong. Just move on and enjoy your own party and your guests will enjoy it too.

The Parties

To paraphrase the lyrics of a show-business anthem, just remember: "Your party is a stage and the stage is a world of entertainment!" When you entertain always make sure it's truly entertaining!

An Elegant Dinner

MENU FOR 8 GUESTS

APERITIF Aviation Cocktail

TO BE PASSED South African Peppadews
With Goat Cheese Filling

Beet Tartar with Feta Cheese
Served on Crispy Spoon-shaped Crackers

FIRST COURSE Fillet of Sea Bass "en Papillote"
With Lemon Kalamata Olive Butter and

Heirloom Tomato and Basil Confit

Served with a basket of crispies, to include "The Kitchen" Cheese Toast

and Phyllo Twists

ENTRÉE American Lamb Fillet
With Fresh Mint Pistou, Lemon Beurre Blanc, and a Baby Vegetable Mélange

Served with a basket of assorted bread rolls

DESSERT Pineapple Carpaccio
With Basil Gelato and Toasted Hazelnuts

Dinner by Candlelight

For a truly special occasion we often want to create an opulent and sumptuous affair to demonstrate to our guest of honor and our guests just how important we believe they are.

For this dinner we pulled out all the stops and loaded the table with a lavish array of all white flowers and fine china, crystal, and silver. The setting is, appropriately, the former estate of Virginia Robinson, known as the "First Lady of Beverly Hills" in the mid-twentieth century. She was famous for her extravagant parties attended by the world's elite, including famous movie stars of the period like Fred Astaire and Charles Boyer. Now a museum bequeathed to Los Angeles County, the historic home is filled with her treasures and the fabulous grounds still possess wonderful gardens that we attempted to emulate indoors.

Two statuesque candelabras mounted with huge arrangements of white garden roses, peonies, dahlias, and hydrangea command the table and rise high above the guests' heads, twining into the overhead crystal chandelier. Down the length of the table, below the guests' eye level, clusters of mixed vintage silver containers are filled with more garden roses, lily of the valley, and sweet peas and each folded linen napkin is decorated with a dainty nosegay of white lavender which is braided with delicate white satin ribbon. The sparkling crystal and silver are complemented by jewel-studded place cards with each guest's name inscribed in graceful calligraphy. Of course we also include as many decorative votive candles as we can fit on the table to cast a flattering golden glow on the happy faces of our guests.

left Each folded napkin is studded with a nosegay of white lavender braided with delicate ribbon.

right An Aviation Cocktail served in a Martini glass perfectly complements this elegant table setting and is the ideal accompaniment to the delicious passed appetizers.

Aviation Cocktail
MAKES 1 DRINK
2 fl oz. gin
1 fl oz. maraschino liqueur
½ oz. freshly squeezed lemon juice
a twist of lemon zest, to garnish

Shake all the ingredients over ice and strain into a chilled Martini glass. Garnish with the lemon zest.

South African Peppadews with Goat Cheese Filling
MAKES 24 OR MORE APPETIZERS
24 pickled peppadews (or other pickled sweet red pepper), drained
½ lb. soft chèvre (goat cheese)
¼ cup finely chopped chives

Drain the peppadews and fill each one with a teaspoon or more of chèvre. Sprinkle with chives. The filled peppadews may be covered and refrigerated for up to 2 hours before serving.

Beet Tartar with Feta Cheese
MAKES 24 OR MORE APPETIZERS
1 lb. red and yellow beets, scrubbed and rinsed
6 tablespoons olive oil
2–3 tablespoons white balsamic vinegar
1 tablespoon Dijon mustard
2 shallots, finely minced
3 tablespoons chopped chives
2 teaspoons dried hot red pepper flakes
¾ cup feta cheese
sea salt and freshly ground black pepper
5 sprigs thyme, leaves removed, for garnish
24 Crispy Spoon-shaped Crackers, to serve (see page 144) or other crackers
aluminum foil

Preheat the oven to 425°F. Toss the beets with 3 tablespoons of the oil and a little salt. Wrap the beets in foil and place them on a baking sheet.

Bake in the preheated oven until they can be easily pierced with a fork, about 1 hour. When cool enough to handle, peel and cut into small dice. Combine the remaining 3 tablespoons oil, vinegar, mustard, shallots, chives, and dried hot red pepper flakes. Toss the cooked beets in the dressing and season to taste with salt and pepper.

Place a teaspoon of feta on a Crispy Spoon-shaped Cracker (see page 144). Top with a tablespoon of the dressed beets. Garnish with a little fresh thyme and serve immediately.

Preheat the oven to 350°F. Place the packets on baking sheets, making sure they are not touching each other. Allow enough space for the paper to puff up. Bake in the preheated oven for 10–12 minutes or until golden brown. Using scissors, cut open the packages in the uncrimped portion. Remove the cooked herbs. Add fresh sprigs of herbs, a little more Lemon Kalamata Olive Butter and a lemon wedge.

Note: The "papillote" is an easy prepared first course. If you want to serve it as an entrée, a few cooked Pee-wee potatoes can be added to the package as you prepare them. After the packages are opened, tuck in steamed asparagus spears or haricot vert.

TOMATO AND BASIL CONFIT
MAKES 4 CUPS
1 medium yellow onion, roughly chopped
3 tablespoons olive oil
1–1½ lb. ripe heirloom tomatoes, peeled
    and chopped
1 cup pitted black olives, chopped
⅓ cup capers
1 cup fresh basil, chiffonade
coarse salt and freshly ground black pepper

In a sauté pan over medium heat, sauté the onion in oil until translucent. Remove from the heat and transfer to a large bowl. Add the tomatoes, olives, capers, basil, and season to taste with salt and pepper.

LEMON KALAMATA OLIVE BUTTER
MAKES 1½ CUPS
2 sticks butter
2 tablespoons finely grated lemon zest
½ cup pitted black kalamata olives, chopped
4 tablespoons thyme or savory, finely chopped

Combine all the ingredients in a food processor and blend until well combined. The butter will keep for 2–3 days in a sealable air-tight container and refrigerated for 2–3 days. Allow to soften before using.

Note: The butter is also food for finishing potatoes or cooked vegetables. Melt a pat on the hot food and toss gently to coat.

Fillet of Sea Bass "en Papillote" with Lemon Kalamata Olive Butter and Heirloom Tomato and Basil Confit
SERVES 8
½ cup olive oil
8 sea bass, sole, or snapper fillets, 6–7 oz. each
Heirloom Tomato and Basil Confit (see right)
Lemon Kalamata Olive Butter (see right), or
    black truffle oil
2 eggs, beaten with 3 tablespoons cold water
sea salt and freshly ground black pepper
16 sprigs thyme, savory, or chervil, to garnish
8 pieces of parchment paper, 12 x 14 inches,
folded and cut into ½ hearts

Open out the parchment paper heart. Brush with olive oil and season with salt and pepper. Place a fish fillet on the right-hand side of the heart and top with 2 tablespoons each of Heirloom Tomato Confit and Lemon Kalamata Olive Butter, or brush with a little black truffle oil.

Fold the left-hand side over the fish and, starting at the top of the heart shape, fold both edges of parchment together to seal, overlapping the folds as you move along. Secure the packet by sharply twisting the end. Brush the outside of the packet with the egg wash. Refrigerate until ready to bake. Repeat with the remaining fish fillets.

American Lamb Fillet with Fresh Mint Pistou, Lemon Beurre Blanc, and a Baby Vegetable Mélange
(see photograph on page 22)
SERVES 8

olive oil, to sear
3 lb. lamb fillet, cleaned and trimmed
¼ cup butter
1½ cups fava beans, cleaned and blanched
1½ cups French radish, cut in half vertically
1½ cups asparagus tips, blanched
1½ cups green and yellow baby summer squash, cut in half and blanched
2 cups Pee-wee or Marble potatoes, blanched
sea salt and freshly ground black pepper
fresh green herbs of your choice, to garnish

To serve:
Fresh Mint Pistou (optional)
Lemon Beurre Blanc (optional)

Preheat the oven to 375°F. Heat sufficient olive oil in a skillet and sear the lamb fillets. Season with salt and pepper. Transfer to a roasting pan and cook in the preheated oven for 20–25 minutes, or until a thermometer inserted in the meat reads 120–125°F. Remove from the oven and let rest for at least 5 minutes.

Melt the butter in a large sauté pan. Add the vegetables and sauté until heated through and tender. Distribute the vegetables between 8 serving plates and top each with 3–4 slices of the lamb. Spoon a little Lemon Beurre Blanc over each serving, if using. Garnish with fresh herbs and serve with a dish of Mint Pistou for passing, if desired.

FRESH MINT PISTOU
MAKES 2–3 CUPS

1 quart packed fresh mint leaves
1 cup coarsely chopped parsley
2 garlic cloves
½ cup grated Parmesan or Asiago cheese
½ cup pine nuts
olive oil to taste
finely grated zest of 1 unwaxed lemon
freshly squeezed lemon juice, to taste
sea salt and freshly ground black pepper

Place the herbs, garlic, cheese, and pine nuts in a food processor. While running, slowly add olive oil until the pistou has the desired consistency. Season with salt and pepper. Add lemon juice and zest to taste.

LEMON BEURRE BLANC
MAKES 1 CUP

½ cup dry white wine
¼ cup shallots, minced
3 tablespoons freshly squeezed lemon juice
2 tablespoons heavy whipping cream
½ cup unsalted butter, cubed
1½ teaspoons finely grated lemon zest
sea salt and freshly ground black pepper

Put the wine and shallots in a saucepan with the lemon juice. Bring to a boil over medium/high heat, and let reduce to about ⅓ cup. Add the cream and continue to boil gently until thickened, about 5 minutes.

Remove the pan from the heat and add the butter a few cubes at a time, whisking until just melted and incorporated into the sauce. Stir in the lemon zest and season to taste with salt and pepper. Keep warm until ready to serve.

Pineapple Carpaccio with Basil Gelato and Toasted Hazelnuts
SERVES 8–10

1 fresh pineapple, peeled
1 cup toasted hazelnuts

For the gelato:
2 cups whole milk
¾ cup heavy cream
1½ cups granulated sugar
¾ cup chopped basil
8 egg yolks
an ice cream maker
2 baking sheets lined with parchment paper

To make the gelato, put the milk, cream, and 1 cup of the sugar in a large saucepan. Bring to a full boil, stirring constantly. Remove the pan from the heat and add the chopped basil immediately. Let the mixture steep for 1 hour or more.

Beat the egg yolks and remaining sugar with an electric mixer until pale yellow. Add the milk mixture and heat in a double boiler, whisking constantly until the mixture thickens. Remove from the heat and pass through a nylon strainer. Chill for several hours or overnight. Follow the manufacturer's instructions for your ice cream maker to finish the ice cream.

To make the Pineapple Carpaccio preheat the oven to 300°F. Slice the pineapple as thinly as possible using an electric slicer or mandoline. Lay out on baking sheets lined with parchment paper. Place in the preheated oven for 15–25 minutes, turning occasionally, until dry, but still pliable.

To serve, fold a slice of pineapple into a cup or flower shape. Add a scoop of the basil gelato and sprinkle with toasted hazelnuts. Serve immediately.

An Asian Inspired Dinner

MENU FOR 6–8 GUESTS

APERITIF	Double Happiness
TO BE PASSED	Wild Mushroom Gyoza
	With Spicy Thai Sauce
	Sashimi Salmon Rice Rolls
	With Wasabi Caviar
FIRST COURSE	Spicy Asian Coleslaw
	With Crispy Fried Ginger and Peanuts
SECOND COURSE	Fillet of Sea Bass in a Ti Leaf Package
	With Ponzu Sauce and Red and Yellow Bell Pepper Sauté,
	Served with a Steamed Jasmine Rice
	Three Pea Mélange
	With Orange Zest
DESSERT	Ginger Tarts
	With Candied Ginger

"*When it comes to flowers, Mark's Garden is the one place Hollywood turns to for that perfect blend of elegance, imagination, and allure, making their creations so unforgettable.*"

Bonnie Tiegel
Producer for Entertainment Tonight

A Tranquil Mood

Much like the art of "bonsai" which originated in China but has become associated with Japan, our Asian party is a blend of Far Eastern motifs and foods. Our objective was to establish a tranquil, Zen-like mood for which we adopted the yin-yang balance of black and white and the natural green hues of nature. The trick is to maintain a calm simplicity in the design but to establish a festive enough ambience that guests still feel they are at a party. We think these two fanciful handmade bonsai trees arching over the table set the perfect tone.

The bonsai trees are made of found tree branches with clumps of Ming greenery attached in bonsai-style clusters. At their feet are mood moss and our signature "glamellias," which for this theme are composed of green cymbidium orchid petals. At first glance a glamellia resembles an oversized natural bloom but it is actually a handmade blossom painstakingly created by attaching individual petals to a central base, most often plastic foam. You will see other versions of this "flower" included in some of our other parties.

A bold patterned black and white runner is a nice blend of simple style and flamboyance to add vitality to the room. Elegant "black" and white calla lilies packed into alternating black and white square glass vases are placed down the center of the table. Some of the calla lily stems are wrapped around the outside of the vase and secured with decorative twine. Votive candles are wrapped in large white calla lily petals and tied with lengths of thin black ribbon. Some small decorative Buddha heads have been placed on the table and each guest's name is written in Japanese script on a place card at each setting to further embody the Asian character of the party.

Double Happiness

MAKES 6-8 DRINKS

4 fl oz. sake
4 fl oz. fresh peach juice or
3 fl oz. peach nectar mixed with 1 fl oz. water
fresh peach slices, to garnish

Pour the sake and peach juice into
a cocktail shaker filled with plenty of
ice. Shake to combine then strain into
chilled cocktail glasses. Garnish each one
with a peach slice and serve immediately.

Wild Mushroom Gyoza with Spicy Thai Sauce

MAKES 35 PIECES

¼ cup vegetable or chicken broth,
   plus 5 tablespoons
⅓ cup oyster sauce
3 tablespoons soy sauce
2 tablespoons unseasoned rice vinegar
2½ tablespoons dry sherry
½ teaspoon sugar
⅛ teaspoon freshly ground black pepper
3–4 tablespoons corn oil
1 tablespoon finely minced fresh ginger
2 tablespoons finely minced garlic
1 yellow onion, finely diced
2 shallots, minced
2 lb. mixed mushrooms, very finely diced
½ cup finely chopped chives
1½ cups thinly sliced scallions
3 tablespoons cornstarch
35 wonton skins

½ cup corn or vegetable oil, for frying
Spicy Thai Sauce, to serve

Put ¼ cup broth plus the next 6 ingredients
in a bowl and whisk to combine. Set aside
until needed.

In a large sauté pan, heat 3 tablespoons oil
and add the ginger and garlic. Sauté over
medium/low heat for about 30 seconds.
Add the onion and shallots and continue to
sauté for 2 minutes more, or until the onions
are translucent. Add the mushrooms and
sauté for another 2–3 minutes, adding more
oil if needed. Add the chives and scallions
and stir in the ingredients in the bowl.
Bring to a simmer. Mix the remaining broth
with the cornstarch and add to the sauté
pan. Stir constantly and bring back to a low
boil to thicken the mushroom mixture. When
thick, remove from heat and allow to cool.

Lay out the wonton skins and place a
tablespoon of the mushroom mixture in the
center of each one. Brush the edges of
the wonton skins with water, fold in half and
press the ends together to seal. Heat the
½ cup oil in a deep, lidded skillet. Place the
gyoza in the pan and brown the bottoms
only. Reduce the heat to medium/low, spray
the tops of gyoza with water or add ½ cup
water. Cover and steam for a minute or two
until completely cooked. Serve immediately
with Spicy Thai sauce.

SPICY THAI SAUCE

MAKES 2½ CUPS

¾ cup corn oil
½ cup rice vinegar
½ cup teriyaki glaze
¼ cup soy sauce
¼ cup sesame oil
2 tablespoons sugar
sambal or other hot sauce, to taste
finely chopped fresh chives, to serve (optional)

Put all of the ingredients in a bowl and
whisk to combine. The dressing will keep
in a sealed jar for 2–3 weeks, refrigerated.
Shake to combine ingredients before using
and add a few chives just before serving.

Sashimi Salmon Rice Rolls with Wasabi Caviar

MAKES 32 APPETIZERS

8 rice paper wrappers
14–16 oz. wild salmon fillet
8 oz. purchased wasabi caviar (optional)
3–4 scallions, cut into 2-inch lengths
bottled plum sauce or sweet chili sauce, to serve

For the filling:

½ cup finely julienned raw carrots
½ cup finely julienned jicama
¼ cup chopped cilantro
2 tablespoons chopped mint
¼ cup bottled plum sauce or sweet chili sauce
1 tablespoon sesame oil
3 tablespoons Thai fish sauce
2 tablespoons grated fresh ginger root

¼ cup roasted and salted peanuts, chopped
¼ cup freshly squeezed lime juice
32 cilantro sprigs, to garnish

Cut each rice paper wrapper into fourths and cut off the rounded edges. Slice the salmon as thinly as possible using a very sharp knife. Combine all the filling ingredients, saving the cilantro sprigs. Soak the rice paper squares in water until pliable then pat dry. Place a cilantro sprig on a rice paper square, top with salmon and a tablespoon of the filling mixture. Roll up tightly like a cigar. Garnish each roll with a teaspoon of wasabi caviar, if using, and a scallion length. Serve immediately with plum sauce or sweet chili sauce for dipping.

Spicy Asian Coleslaw

SERVES 8–10

freshly squeezed juice of 1 orange
freshly squeezed juice of 2 limes
1 tablespoon sugar
2 tablespoons rice vinegar
¼ cup vegetable oil
a pinch of sea salt
3 tablespoons bottled sweet chili sauce
1 tablespoon hot sauce, or to taste
1 Napa cabbage, finely shredded
1 medium head red cabbage, shredded
½ head Savoy cabbage, shredded
2 carrots, grated (about ½ cup)
½ jicama, peeled and cut into thin matchsticks
4 Persian cucumbers, thinly sliced
1½ cups mint leaves, shredded

1½ cups pickled ginger, well drained
2 cups salted peanuts
oil, for shallow frying

To make the dressing put the first 8 ingredients in a small bowl and whisk to combine. Place the Napa cabbage, red cabbage, Savoy cabbage, carrots, jicama, cucumbers, and mint in a large salad bowl. Heat a little oil in a wok. Fry the ginger until crispy. Remove from the pan with a slotted spoon and drain on paper towels.

To assemble the salad, add the fried ginger and peanuts to the cabbage mixture, pour in the dressing and toss the salad to distribute evenly. Serve immediately.

Fillet of Sea Bass in a Ti Leaf Package with Ponzu Sauce and Red and Yellow Bell Pepper Sauté

SERVES 8

9 fresh Ti leaves
8 x 6–7 oz. sea bass or halibut fillets
3 red and yellow bell peppers, julienned
2 tablespoons olive oil
sea salt and freshly ground black pepper
2 cups Ponzu Sauce, to serve (see right)
steamed jasmine rice, to serve (optional)

Simmer the Ti leaves in a large pan of boiling water until pliable. Pat dry with paper towels. Pull a Ti leaf into 8 long shreds and set aside with the remaining Ti leaves.

Lightly sauté the peppers in olive oil. Season the fish fillets and lightly brown on both sides in a hot grill pan. On each Ti leaf, place a fish fillet, ¼ cup Ponzu Sauce, and a few sautéed red and yellow peppers. Fold and wrap each Ti leaf to form a package and tie shut with one of the Ti leaf shreds. Refrigerate until ready to cook.

Preheat the oven to 375°F. Spread the Ti leaf and fish packages on baking sheets. Bake in the preheated oven for 25 minutes, or until the fish is tender and the leaf slightly browned. Serve with steamed jasmine rice and additional Ponzu Sauce for pouring.

PONZU SAUCE

MAKES 2½ CUPS

½ cup freshly squeezed lemon juice
1 cup rice vinegar
¾ cups soy sauce
¼ cup mirin (sweet cooking sake) or
    dry sherry
freshly grated zest of 2 unwaxed lemon

Combine all the ingredients in a saucepan
and bring to a boil, stirring continuously.
Let cool and refrigerate until needed.

Three Pea Mélange with Orange Zest

SERVES 8

1 lb. frozen peas, defrosted, or 2 cups shelled
    fresh peas (about 4 cups in the shell)
1 lb. sugar snaps, trimmed
1 lb. snow peas, trimmed
2 tablespoons olive oil or butter
¼ cup freshly squeezed orange juice
sea salt and freshly ground black pepper
2 tablespoons freshly grated orange zest

In a large skillet, heat the oil or butter. Add
the peas, sugar snaps, and snow peas and
sauté for 1–2 minutes. Add the orange juice
and continue to sauté until heated through
but still a little crunchy. Season with salt and
pepper. Sprinkle with orange zest to serve.

Ginger Tarts

MAKES 8 INDIVIDUAL TARTS

For the tart shell:
1 lb. prepared shortbread cookies, ground into
    fine crumbs
½ cup sugar
freshly grated zest from 2 unwaxed lemons
6 tablespoons cold unsalted butter, cut into pieces
2 teaspoons ground ginger

For the filling:
4 tablespoons milk
3 teaspoons unflavored gelatin
1 cup finely chopped candied ginger, plus extra
    finely julienned to garnish
½ cup sugar
2 teaspoons freshly squeezed lemon juice
1½ teaspoons salt
4 cups heavy cream
1½ cups crème fraîche

8 x 5-inch round tart pans with false bottoms

Preheat the oven to 350°F. To make the
tart shells, combine the shortbread crumbs,
sugar, lemon zest, butter, and ginger in
a food processor until it starts to come
together. Line the tart pans with the dough,
pressing it down on the base and into the
sides. Place on baking sheets and bake in
the preheated oven for 15 minutes, until
golden. Remove from the oven and set
aside to cool.

To make the filling, put the milk in a bowl,
sprinkle the gelatin over the top, and let it
soften. Transfer the mixture to a saucepan
and cook with the ginger, sugar, lemon
juice, salt, and 2 cups of the cream. Stir over
medium heat until the gelatin and sugar are
dissolved. Remove from the heat and let
cool to room temperature.

In a large bowl, whisk the crème fraîche
until it is smooth. Whip the remaining 2 cups
heavy cream to soft peaks and gently fold
into the crème fraîche. Gently fold the ginger
milk mixture into the whipped cream until
combined. Spoon the mixture into the tart
shells and chill in the refrigerator until set.

When ready to serve, carefully remove the
tarts from the pans and sprinkle the top of
each one with a little candied ginger.

A Summertime Lunch

MENU FOR 6–8 GUESTS

APERITIF	Fresh Peach Fuzz
APPETIZER	Chilled Tomato Soup
	Served in glasses and with Basil Oil and Fresh Basil Garnish
ENTRÉE	Sharp Cheddar Cheese Soufflés
	Served with Cheddar Cheese Sauce with White Truffle Oil
DESSERT	Red Berry Romanoff
	With Grand Marnier Romanoff Sauce
	Lace Cookies

right Big, luscious hydrangea blooms float in glass lanterns hanging from the tree limbs. *below right* Passion flower blooms add an exotic touch.

Summer Breeze

To escape the summer heat our summertime lunch is set at a long table on the lawn under a sprawling shade tree. To complement our light summer menu we have chosen a color palette predominantly of blues to provide a cool, soothing environment. After enjoying a frosty Peach Fuzz drink or a glass of icy lemonade on the veranda, our guests will move to the table bathed in a sea of shimmering blue and lavender flowers to settle in for an afternoon of "easy living."

Every blue and lavender flower we could lay our hands on is incorporated into this tabletop to soothe the soul and please the senses. Hydrangea provides us with a wonderful variety of blue tones to which we have added hyacinth, muscari, a few purple callas and tulips, and one of our favorites straight from the garden—passion vine. This is all generously spread out over a patterned tablecloth to match the expected mood of the gathering. The chair backs are also treated with hydrangea and the big, luscious blooms float in glass lanterns hanging from the tree limbs. As a party favor guests will take home the loose nosegays that adorn the silver epergne in the center of the table.

Fresh Peach Fuzz
MAKES 4-6 DRINKS
½ a 12 fl oz. container frozen lemonade
    concentrate (do not dilute)
6 fl oz. gin or vodka
2-3 ripe peaches, unpeeled and sliced
4-5 ice cubes
mint sprigs to garnish

Combine all the ingredients in a blender,
saving some peach slices to garnish. Purée
at high speed until smooth. Adjust to taste.
Garnish with mint and the reserved peach
slices. Serve immediately.

Chilled Tomato Soup
SERVES 8-10
4 lbs. ripe plum tomatoes
8 cloves garlic, peeled
leaves from 4 sprigs of thyme
⅓ cup olive oil
2 cucumbers, peeled and chopped
½ cup sun-dried tomatoes in olive oil
6 cups chicken or vegetable stock
sea salt and freshly ground black pepper
basil oil and basil leaves, to garnish
2 baking sheets with a rim
8–10 Martini glasses or similar

Preheat the oven to 350°F. Chop the
tomatoes and combine with the garlic and
thyme. Toss in olive oil and spread on the
baking sheets. Roast in the preheated oven
for 45–60 minutes. Remove from the oven
and allow to cool.

Put the cooked tomato mixture, cucumbers,
and tomatoes in a food processor. Blend to
a purée and add the stock. Season to taste
with salt and pepper. Chill for several hours
or overnight.

Serve in Martini glasses or icers, drizzled
with basil oil and garnished with fresh basil.

Sharp Cheddar Cheese Soufflés
SERVES 8-10
3 tablespoons unsalted butter, plus extra
    for greasing
¼ cup finely grated Parmesan cheese,
    plus extra for sprinkling
¼ cup all-purpose flour
1 cup scalded milk
a pinch of cayenne pepper
a pinch of nutmeg
4 extra large egg yolks, at room temperature
5 oz. extra sharp cheddar cheese, shredded
5 extra large egg whites, at room temperature
⅛ teaspoon cream of tartar
Kosher salt and freshly ground black pepper
8–10 individual soufflé dishes or ramekins

Preheat the oven to 375°F. Butter the soufflé
dishes and sprinkle with Parmesan. Melt the
butter in a small saucepan over low heat.
Stir in the flour and cook for 2 minutes,
stirring constantly. Remove from the heat,
whisk in the hot milk, ½ teaspoon each of
salt and pepper, the cayenne and nutmeg.
Cook over low heat, beating constantly, for
1 minute until smooth and thick.

Remove from the heat. While still hot, whisk
in the egg yolks, one at a time. Stir in the
cheddar and ½ cup Parmesan. Transfer to
a large bowl.

In a separate bowl, use an electric whisk to
whisk the egg whites, cream of tartar, and
a pinch of salt on low speed for 1 minute,
medium for 1 minute, and then high, until
they form firm, glossy peaks.

Whisk half the egg whites into the cheese
mixture to lighten it, then fold in the rest.
Pour into the prepared soufflé dishes. Bake
in the preheated oven for 30–35 minutes
until puffed and brown. Serve immediately
with warm Cheddar Cheese Sauce with
White Truffle Oil.

CHEDDAR CHEESE SAUCE WITH WHITE TRUFFLE OIL

Makes about 1 quart

¼ cup butter
¼ cup all-purpose flour
2½ cups milk or half-and-half
1 teaspoon Worcestershire sauce
2 cups sharp cheddar cheese, shredded
1–2 teaspoons white truffle oil, plus extra
  to season
salt and freshly ground black pepper

In a medium saucepan, melt the butter and stir in the flour. Cook over low heat for about 2 minutes, until a golden brown. Remove from the heat and add the milk, Worcestershire sauce, cheese, and white truffle oil. Return to the heat and stir continuously until the cheese has melted and all the ingredients have combined to make a smooth sauce. Season to taste with salt, pepper, and a little more truffle oil if desired. Serve warm or gently reheat before serving.

Red Berry Romanoff

SERVES 8–10

8 oz. each of blueberries, blackberries,
  raspberries, and strawberries
½ cup granulated sugar
¼ cup Grand Marnier
Grand Marnier Romanoff Sauce, to serve
Lace Biscuits, to serve (optional)
8–10 individual serving glasses

Rinse all of the berries and hull and slice the strawberries. Put them in a large bowl, sprinkle with sugar and pour in the Grand Marnier. Stir gently to coat and set aside to let the sugar dissolve in the Grand Marnier.

When ready to serve, spoon a generous amount of berries into serving glasses. Top with Grand Marnier Romanoff Sauce and garnish with a Lace Cookie, if desired.

GRAND MARNIER ROMANOFF SAUCE

MAKES about 1 quart

6 egg yolks
1 cup granulated sugar
1½ cups heavy cream
¼ cup Grand Marnier liqueur

Put the egg yolks in a metal mixing bowl and whisk. Slowly whisk in the sugar until the mixture is a pale yellow and the sugar has dissolved. Place the mixture over a double boiler, and whisk over low heat until thick. Let cool.

Put the cream in a large bowl and whip to stiff peaks. Fold the whipped cream and Grand Marnier into the cooled egg and sugar mixture.

Note: "The Kitchen" also serve this sauce as a dip with a platter of fresh fruit.

Lace Cookies

SERVES 8–10

½ cup butter
½ cup sugar
⅓ cup dark corn syrup
½ cup flour
1 teaspoon ground ginger
½ teaspoon salt
a baking sheet, lightly greased

Preheat the oven to 375°F. Put the butter, sugar, and corn syrup in a saucepan and cook over medium heat, stirring continuously, for 4 minutes. Add the flour, ginger, and salt and whisk or stir until well combined. Remove from the heat and let cool. Transfer the mixture to a storage container and chill in the refrigerator for several hours or until set.

Once set, use two teaspoons or a small ice cream scoop to transfer mounds of the mixture to the prepared baking sheet. Bake until the mixture spreads and is golden brown, about 15 minutes. Let cool slightly but, while still warm, cut or mold into desired shapes. The cookies will keep for up to 1 week stored in an airtight container. Use as a garnish for Red Berry Romanoff with Grand Marnier Romanoff sauce or serve with ice cream.

below Even the lemonade station that stands nearby is circled with hydrangea and tufts of muscari, giving our guests the feeling they are swept by a cooling breeze.

High Style

The British invented the cocktail party (reportedly the author Alec Waugh in the 1920s) but it was probably the Americans who really perfected the art of cocktail mixing. Apparently during the Prohibition period mixing liquor with other liquids disguised the horrible flavor of bootleg alcohol. Although once out of fashion, cocktails today are more stylish than ever and from that we take our cue to raise the art of the cocktail party to the highest level of chic. Elegant black and white with a splash of yellow is what we have chosen to establish a mood of sophistication along with the unexpected.

Because yellow is an "edgy" color and works well as an accent, we like this combination along with the perfect complacency of black and white. Sleek, stark, and sophisticated, this is a dramatic setting for the most glamorous array of guests. Even the most modest can feel exceptional in this environment. Masses of black calla lilies, yellow freesia, and yellow craspedia balls accented with large tropical leaves and trimmed horsetail become sculptural art pieces in this gorgeous showcase of light and shadow. Can't you just imagine Audrey Hepburn standing in the corner in a black cocktail dress?

A Birthday Cake Party

MENU FOR 8-10 GUESTS

APERITIF	French 75
FIRST COURSE TRIO	Wild Mushroom Bisque
	Watercress, Baby Arugula, and Mizuni Green Salad
	With Walnut Vinaigrette, Toasted Walnuts, and Edible Flowers
	Phyllo Twists
	With Wild Mushroom and Fontina Cheese Filling
ENTRÉE	Asparagus Ravioli
	With a Ricotta Cheese and Asparagus Filling
	And a Topping of Baby Asparagus Tips, Fava Beans, Fresh Peas, Lemon Zest,
	Orange Curls, and Parmesan Cheese Curls
DESSERT	Chocolate Fudge Cake
	With Chocolate Buttercream and Decorated with Chocolate Leaves

Surprise Party

above Each cake is a unique creation using roses, orchid petals, tropical flowers, carnations, and leaves, with fresh fruit accents to produce an extraordinary cross between an actual birthday cake and a traditional floral centerpiece.

At this party, the birthday cakes make it a real "surprise party" for your guests because the cakes ARE the decoration. Although these cakes look good enough to eat they are made of flowers and are so fascinating that nobody would even think of cutting into one. We use a wide array of bright and happy floral colors to set the mood for fun. Our hanging "chandeliers" are faux gift packages wrapped in contrasting colors and strung together from the crossbars of the arbor to hover amusingly over the table. Such an exceptional display as this calls for an equally unusual table covering so we gathered ribbons in similar festive colors and interlaced them into this fanciful top mixing solids, polka dots, stripes, and plaids with great abandon. This lighthearted and playful decoration matches the relaxed setting under this delightful backyard arbor and the delicate but satisfying menu.

left Each place setting features an individual floral cupcake in its own fabric wrapped box as a take-home memory of this fun day.

"Celebrations, congratulations, condolences, those occasions that involve the phrases 'I love you' and 'I'm sorry'—at every event and every moment in my life that requires flowers, Mark's Garden is in the picture. By now, the folks there know what we want and need, even better than we do. And we're talking about the last fifteen years! Simply put, Mark's Garden is part of my life." **John Lithgow**

French 75

MAKES 1 DRINK

1 fl oz. gin
¾ fl oz. sugar syrup (see page 73)
½ fl oz. freshly squeezed lemon juice
chilled Champagne
lemon rind spiral for garnish
1 French sugar cube

Shake the first three ingredients well with ice and strain into a chilled Champagne glass. Top with Champagne and garnish with lemon rind and a French sugar cube.

Wild Mushroom Bisque

MAKES 6 CUPS

1½ lbs. various wild mushrooms, or button mushrooms
2 slices bacon, chopped
1 cup chopped white onion
2 cloves garlic, chopped
¼ cup brandy
½ cup white wine
3 cups chicken stock
1½ cups whipping cream
oil, for frying
sea salt and freshly ground black pepper

Clean the mushrooms with a damp paper towel or cloth and chop finely.

Put the bacon in a skillet and sauté over medium heat (without extra fat) for 2–3 minutes. Add the onion, garlic, and mushrooms. Continue to sauté until the mushrooms begin to brown. Add the brandy and wine and simmer until most of the liquid has evaporated. Add the chicken stock and continue to simmer, stirring occasionally, for 15 minutes. Let cool.

Transfer the mixture to a blender in batches and process until smooth. Pour into a large bowl and stir in the cream. Season to taste with salt and pepper. Cover the bowl or transfer to a sealable container and refrigerate until ready to use. Reheat gently and serve.

Note: A few raw enoki mushrooms or slices of sautéed mushrooms are a good topping. Crumbled crisp-fried bacon and snipped chives could also enhance the soup.

Watercress, Baby Arugula, and Mizuni Green Salad

SERVES 8-10

2 cups watercress
2 cups baby arugula
2 cups mizuni
1 cup toasted walnuts
edible flowers for garnish (optional)
sea salt and freshly ground pepper

For the Walnut Vinaigrette:
¾ cup Champagne vinegar, plus extra to taste
2 tablespoons Dijon mustard
2 tablespoons brown sugar
1 tablespoon minced shallots
¼ cup toasted walnuts
¾ cup walnut oil
¼ cup olive oil

First make the Walnut Vinaigrette. Put all the ingredients, except for the olive oil, in a blender or food processor. Pulse to roughly combine, then turn on. While the machine is running, add the olive oil in a slow steady stream to emulsify. Add seasoning to taste.

A Fantasy Picnic

MENU FOR 6-8 GUESTS

APERITIF Pineapple Mint Julep

DINNER Spanish Almond Deviled Eggs
With Toasted Marcona Almonds

Crispy Fried Panko Chicken
With Fresh Peach Chutney

Haricots Verts and Asparagus
With Yellow Cherry Tomatoes and a Citrus Vinaigrette

Mâche, Arugula, and Endive Salad
With a Champagne Vinaigrette

"The Kitchen's" Potato Salad
With Peas and Bacon

DESSERT Apricot Oatmeal Bars

left Provence in the era of
the French impressionists is the
inspiration for this idealized picnic.

French Impressions

A private wooded road leading from our friend's home in Pasadena provides a perfect fantasy setting for a secluded "country" picnic while remaining close to the city. We chose a fresh mixture of purple and golden tones, including sunflowers and lavender in willow baskets to evoke the mood of Provence and the great Impressionist painters. The dappled sunlight glistening through the trees reinforces that effect. However we move toward to a more sophisticated ambience than purely rustic by adding some vintage china, silver, and crystal on a Battenberg lace tablecloth to complement our up-scaled lunch menu.

Rustic baskets packed with mixed varieties of sunflowers and cut lavender are set on the dining table and the picnic buffet. We placed tiny bouquets of cut lavender tied with a delicate lavender ribbon on each napkin and pinned sprigs to the lace tablecloth. We even gathered planted pots of coreopsis, blackeyed susan, and Dutch iris around us to add more color to the area, proving you can sometimes improve on nature by adding more nature! And if you look closely in the background, you can even see our prized handmade bench of birch branches for additional seating.

A Romantic Dinner for Two

MENU FOR 2

APERITIF	Rose Petal Martini
FIRST COURSE	Artichoke Soup with White Truffle Oil Served in an Artichoke Cup
SECOND COURSE	Beef Tournedo on an Asparagus Raft With a Red Wine Sauce and Crisp Root Vegetable Garnish
DESSERT	Boca Negra Cakes With Hot Fudge Sauce and White Chocolate Cream

True Romance

A gentleman is planning on proposing marriage tonight and he and his friends have gone to great lengths to make it as romantic and sexy an evening as possible. We have found a secluded balcony to allow our couple utmost privacy. By combining red and black we lend a contemporary "gothic" tone to the décor, giving the setting an extra edge of sensuality. The secret, however, is that before placing the champagne to chill in a bucket nearby and lighting the candles on the table, we have hidden a ring box in the top of the floral centerpiece and covered it with roses. The lady may not be completely surprised by the proposal but she will be impressed with the gentleman's ingenuity.

Red roses, of course, are the historical symbol of romance and we are making the most of it. The centerpiece is a gorgeous grouping of mixed shades of red roses studded with and surrounded by glittering jewels for an added touch of glamour. A red striped rose is tucked into a rolled red silk napkin and more red roses "rain" from the candlelit chandelier above the table. More red votive candles are nested in black quartz holders to provide a romantic glow and the setting is displayed on a sheer black organdy appliquéd tabletop placed over red silk.

Rose Petal Martini
MAKES 2 DRINKS
½ cup granulated sugar
⅓ cup vodka
1 tablespoon freshly squeezed lemon juice
1–2 teaspoons prepared rose syrup
fresh rose petals, to garnish

Make a sugar syrup by dissolving the sugar in ¼ cup water in a pan over low heat. Bring to a boil over high heat. Remove the pan from the heat and allow to cool completely.

Combine the vodka, lemon juice, rose syrup, and 3 tablespoons sugar syrup in a cocktail shaker filled with ice. Shake and strain into two well-chilled Martini glasses. Garnish with rose petals.

Artichoke Soup with White Truffle Oil
SERVES 8–10
5 artichokes (or one 14-oz. can artichoke bottoms)
½ cup butter
1 cup chopped shallots or onion
7 cups chicken or vegetable stock
1 cup dry white wine
½ lb. potatoes, peeled and diced
1 cup heavy cream
white truffle oil, to taste
sea salt and freshly ground black pepper
vegetable or potato chips, to serve (optional)

For the steamed artichoke cups:
2 large globe artichokes
a bunch of thyme
sea salt and freshly ground black pepper

To make the artichoke cups, use a sharp knife to cut the top ½ inch from the artichokes and trim off the stems. Using scissors, cut the pointed edges off each leaf. Place the artichoke bottoms up in a steamer, adding the thyme, salt and pepper. Cover and cook for 30–40 minutes. When an outer leaf pulls away easily or a fork, is easily inserted in the center, the artichoke is cooked. Drain the artichokes upside down until cool. Using a large spoon, hollow out the centre of each artichoke, so that it is large enough to fit a small cup. This is the cup in which the soup will be served. If necessary, trim the bottoms of each artichoke again, so that they will sit level on a plate. Set aside until needed.

To make the soup, cut the artichokes lengthwise into quarters, and remove and discard the thistly chokes. Remove the leaves, leaving the artichoke hearts and 2 inches of stem. Chop into ¼-inch pieces.

In a large pot, melt the butter and sauté the artichoke bottoms and shallots for about 5 minutes. Add the stock, wine, and potatoes. Simmer until the potatoes and artichokes are tender. Let cool. Purée the soup in a blender or food mill, in batches if necessary. Refrigerate until ready to serve.

When ready to serve, reheat the liquid and whisk in the cream. Season to taste with salt, pepper, and white truffle oil. Ladle into the prepared Artichoke Cups, garnish with a large vegetable or potato chip, and serve immediately. (Leftover soup can be poured into a resealable container and frozen.)

above Stylish and unusual presentation is key to impressive party food. Here, a simple artichoke soup has been served in a cup surrounded by a fresh artichoke, making an attractive serving dish.

Beef Tournedo on an Asparagus Raft

SERVES 2

1 beef tenderloin, cleaned and trimmed
¼ cup butter
1 lb. asparagus spears, trimmed and steamed
sea salt and freshly ground black pepper

RED WINE SAUCE

MAKES 2 CUPS

1 bottle dry red wine (750 ml), plus extra to taste
1 quart beef stock
1 large onion, chopped
2 cloves garlic, minced
1 carrot, chopped
1 tablespoon dry mustard
a few parsley sprigs
½ cup butter, cubed
sea salt and freshly ground black pepper

CRISP ROOT VEGETABLE GARNISH (optional)

3–4 beets, carrots, onions, or parsnips
corn oil, for deep frying
sea salt flakes

First make the red wine sauce. Combine the wine, stock, onion, garlic, carrot, mustard, and parsley in a large saucepan. Bring to just below a boil and simmer until reduced to about 2 cups. Remove from the heat, strain, and refrigerate. When ready to serve, reheat the sauce, whisking in the butter in small pieces until the sauce thickens. Season to taste with salt and pepper.

To make the crisp root vegetables, trim the tops and bottoms of the beets, carrots, onions, or parsnips. Peel with a vegetable peeler and use a mandoline to slice them lengthwise into long thin strips. Add about 6 inches of oil to a deep-fryer and heat to 350°F. Deep-fry the vegetables for about 2 minutes or until crisp. Place them on paper towels to drain and sprinkle with salt flakes.

To make the tournedos, slice the beef into 8–10 rounds. Save two rounds, and wrap and freeze the remaining beef for another time. Lightly pound the beef with a steak hammer and season with salt and pepper.

Melt 2 tablespoons butter in a heavy skillet and sear the beef on each side. Transfer to a roasting pan. When ready to serve, finish in an oven preheated to 375°F and roast for 8–12 minutes, until a thermometer inserted into the meat reads 115°F and the beef is still pink in the center.

Sauté the asparagus spears in the remaining butter and season to taste. Arrange the asparagus in a "raft" on two warmed serving plates. Put a beef round on top of each. Reheat the red wine sauce and spoon over the top. Garnish with crisp root vegetables, if using, and serve immediately.

Boca Negra Cakes

MAKES 12 SMALL CAKES

12 oz. bittersweet chocolate, coarsely chopped
1⅓ cup sugar
½ cup bourbon
8 oz. unsalted butter, cut into 10 pieces
5 eggs, room temperature
1½ tablespoons all-purpose flour
bittersweet chocolate curls, to garnish
a 12-cup muffin pan, lightly greased
2 x 10-oz. Martini glasses or serving dishes

HOT FUDGE SAUCE

½ cup heavy cream
3 tablespoons unsalted butter, cut into small pieces
⅓ cup granulated sugar
⅓ cup dark brown sugar, firmly packed
a pinch of salt
½ cup sifted unsweetened dutch-process
  cocoa powder

WHITE CHOCOLATE CREAM

(Note: this must be prepared 1 day in advance)
12 oz. white chocolate, finely chopped
1 cup heavy cream
¼ cup bourbon, plus extra to taste
1 cup heavy cream, whipped to stiff peaks

To make the Hot Fudge Sauce, put the cream and butter in a heavy saucepan over medium heat. Stir until the butter is melted and the cream just comes to a low boil. Add both sugars and stir for a few minutes until

they have dissolved. Reduce the heat. Add the salt and cocoa powder and whisk until smooth. Remove from the heat and transfer to a container with a tight-fitting lid. Refrigerate until ready to serve. Reheat in a metal bowl over simmering water, being careful not to let it scorch. (This sauce will keep for 2–3 weeks in the refrigerator.)

To make the White Chocolate Cream, put the white chocolate in the bowl of a food processor fitted with a metal blade, or into a blender. Heat the heavy cream in a small saucepan over medium heat until small bubbles form around the edge of the pan. Pour the cream over the chocolate and blend until completely smooth. Add the bourbon, taste, and add more, if desired. Transfer to a container with a tight-fitting lid and chill overnight. When ready to serve, bring the mixture to room temperature and gradually fold in the whipped cream.

To make the cakes, preheat the oven to 350°F. Put the chopped chocolate in a medium bowl. In a large saucepan, mix 1 cup of the sugar and the bourbon and cook over medium heat, stirring occasionally, until the sugar dissolves and the mixture comes to a full boil. Immediately pour the hot syrup over the chocolate and stir with a wooden spoon, beating in the butter one piece at a time, until well blended.

Beat the eggs until pale yellow. Gradually add the flour to the eggs. Slowly pour the chocolate mixture into the egg mixture, beating constantly. Pour the cake batter into the prepared muffin pan. Bake in the preheated oven for 20–25 minutes. Allow to cool for 5 minutes, then turn out onto a wire rack. Note: once cool, the extra cakes can be frozen and enjoyed another time.

To serve, pour 2 tablespoons reheated Hot Fudge Sauce into each serving glass. Carefully place a cake on top. Top with White Chocolate Cream and garnish with chocolate curls. Serve immediately.

Christmas Nouveau

MENU FOR 8–10

APERITIF	Garnet Slip
TO BE PASSED	Caviar and Smoked Salmon Blini Puffs With Crème Fraîche and Lemon Zest
BUFFET	Celery Root Salad With a Dijon Vinaigrette
	Braised Brussels Sprouts With Pistachio Nuts
	Festive Rice With Leeks, Marcona Almonds, and Morello Cherries
	Pork Roast with Cumberland Sauce With an Apricot, Prune, and Cranberry Stuffing
	Lobster Thermidor Served on a Bed of Rock Salt
	Roasted Cornish Game Hens With Sage Sausage and Mushroom Stuffing
DESSERT	Holiday Bavarian Cream

A Feast for the Eyes

Christmas entertaining is generally about maintaining tradition, but we like to create some new traditions too. Our buffet table in this comfortable California Craftsman home is laden with classic foods with our own variations and some complete surprises like Lobster Thermidor. By the same token, our décor is a new take on the old standbys. We have chosen a deep rich red palette to denote the season and complement the warmth of the dark wood paneling and furniture as well as the colorful displays of food. Antique silver pieces display innovative Christmas trees and "ornaments" that are made of fresh flowers, of course, and fresh fruit.

Our Christmas trees are oversized cones of pavéd large bloom red roses with ornate toppers. Instead of placing traditional ornaments on the trees, we have made some out of flowers and set them on silver pedestals and candle stands. In addition to roses, we have pavéd our Christmas trees and ornamental balls with cherries and raspberries. The red silk napkins are tied with silver tassels to add some sparkle. Tall taper candles mixed with fat pillar candles add a further touch of warmth and hospitality. The overall effect is a feast for the eyes as well as the palate. Eat, drink, and be merry.

Garnet Slip

MAKES 1 DRINK

1 fl oz. vodka

½ fl oz. limoncello (Italian lemon liqueur)

2–3 fl oz. fresh raspberry juice

2–3 fl oz. fresh or canned peach juice or nectar

fresh lemon rind and fresh raspberries, to garnish

a Martini glass rimmed with superfine sugar

Put the vodka, limoncello, and juices in a cocktail shaker and mix well with cracked ice. Strain into a glass. Garnish with lemon rind and raspberries. Serve immediately.

Caviar and Smoked Salmon Blini Puffs

MAKES 24 PUFFS

2 cups cottage cheese

1 tablespoon sour cream

1 teaspoon pure vanilla extract

½ teaspoon sugar

3 tablespoons butter, melted

3 eggs

½ cup flour

1 cup crème fraîche

4 oz. caviar and/or smoked salmon

zest from 1 unwaxed lemon, to garnish

2 x 12-cup mini-muffin pans, buttered

Preheat the oven to 350°F. Put the first 7 ingredients in a food processor and blend until smooth. Pour the batter into the prepared muffin pans and bake in the preheated oven for 12–15 minutes or until golden brown.

To assemble, spoon a small amount of crème fraîche onto each blini, then top with a slice of smoked salmon or small amount of caviar. Garnish with lemon zest.

Note: the puffs may be made ahead of time, frozen, and reheated at 350°F. The Kitchen has found that the blinis are delicious when they are reheated in a deep-fat fryer.

Celery Root Salad

SERVES 8

2 large celery roots, trimmed and peeled, or 4 cups canned celery root, drained

2–3 carrots, cleaned and trimmed

butter lettuce leaves, to serve

DIJON VINAIGRETTE

¼ cup white balsamic vinegar

½ teaspoon salt

2 tablespoons Dijon mustard

¾ cup extra virgin olive oil

2 tablespoons shallots, minced

1 tablespoon black pepper

To make the Dijon Vinaigrette, mix the vinegar, salt, and mustard in a food processor. Slowly add the oil in a steady stream until an emulsion forms. Add the shallots and pepper. Quarter the celery roots. In a food processor, shred them and the carrots with a coarse grating disk. Add the vinaigrette, toss the salad, and serve on a bed of butter lettuce leaves.

Braised Brussels Sprouts

SERVES 8–10

2 lbs. fresh, leafy brussel sprouts

2–3 tablespoons butter or extra virgin olive oil

2 tablespoons minced shallots

¼ cup chicken or vegetable broth

½ cup pistachio nuts, shelled

salt and freshly ground black pepper

Peel the sprouts as far as possible, reserving the leaves. Shred the cores. Melt the butter in a large skillet, add the shallots and sauté for a couple of minutes. Add the brussel sprout leaves and shredded cores and sauté for another minute or two. Add the broth and simmer until the sprouts are tender. Season to taste and top with pistachios.

Festive Rice

SERVES 8

2 cups basmati rice
4 cardamom pods
3 cups sliced leeks, white and light green part only
1 tablespoon olive oil or butter
1 cup Spanish Marcona almonds
1 cup canned or jarred morello cherries, drained
salt and freshly ground black pepper

Wash and drain the rice. Bring 2¾ cups water to a rolling boil. Stir in the rice and a pinch of salt. Return to a boil. Add the cardamom, cover, and reduce heat. Simmer for 15 minutes. Remove from heat and keep covered for 15 minutes. Sauté the leeks in olive oil until soft. Add the almonds and sauté, adding the cherries last. When hot, add to the rice, season to taste, and serve.

Pork Roast with Cumberland Sauce

SERVES 8-10

6–7 lb. pork loin roast, bone in
1 cup dried cranberries
1 cup dried prunes, chopped
1½ cups dried apricots, chopped
1 apple, cored and chopped
1¼ cups Calvados (French apple brandy)
¼ cup unsalted butter
2 cups finely chopped onion
salt and freshly ground black pepper

CUMBERLAND SAUCE

⅓ cup port
⅔ cup freshly squeezed orange juice
1½ tablespoons freshly squeezed lemon juice
¼ cup red-currant jelly
¼ teaspoon ground ginger
¼ teaspoon salt
2 tablespoons cornstarch and 2 tablespoons water
2 tablespoons unsalted butter

Preheat the oven to 375°F. Using a knife or reamer, make a 1–2 inch hole through the center of the loin; set aside. Combine the fruit and Calvados in a bowl and let macerate for an hour. Melt the butter in a skillet. Add the onion and sauté until tender and slightly caramelized. Add the onion and any juices to the fruit, then drain, saving the liquid. Stuff the fruit into the pork, baste with the reserved marinade, and season. Put the pork on a rack and roast in

the preheated oven for 1½ hours or until a thermometer inserted into the meat reads 150°F. Let the pork rest for 15 minutes while you make the sauce.

To make the Cumberland Sauce, skim all but 1 tablespoon fat from the roasting pan. Put the pan across two burners, add ½ cup water, and boil over high heat to deglaze. Scrape up any brown bits. Add the port and boil for 1 minute. Add the orange and lemon juices, jelly, ginger, and salt and whisk until the jelly is dissolved. Whisk together the cornstarch and water in a cup, then add to the pan and simmer, whisking, until the sauce is thickened, about 1 minute. Remove from the heat and whisk in the butter. Pour through a fine-mesh sieve and serve hot.

Lobster Thermidor

SERVES 8

1 cup butter, melted
freshly squeezed juice of 1 lemon
2 tablespoons each of chives and dill, snipped
8–10 lobster tails, meat removed and shells saved

For the sauce:
4 tablespoons unsalted butter
1 white onion, finely chopped
2 tablespoons all-purpose flour
¼ cup dry sherry or white wine
1 cup whipping cream
1 tablespoon paprika
2 tablespoons tomato paste
sea salt and freshly ground black pepper
rock salt, to display (optional)

Preheat the oven to 325°F. Combine the melted butter, lemon juice, chives, and dill. Brush the lobster meat with the butter mixture. Place it in a roasting pan with the lobster shells. Roast in the preheated oven for 25–30 minutes, until the meat is opaque. Remove from the oven, put 1 tablespoon of the remaining butter mixture in the bottom of each shell. Cut the meat into crosswise pieces and return it to the shells. Melt the butter in a skillet, add the onion, and sauté until softened. Add the flour and cook, stirring, until golden brown. Add the sherry, cream, paprika, and tomato paste. Cook until the mixture thickens and season to taste. Arrange the lobster tails over rock salt, ladle over the sauce and serve immediately.

Roasted Cornish Game Hens

SERVES 8

8 Cornish game hens, boned
2 tablespoons butter or extra virgin olive oil
2 cups onions, chopped
2 lbs. sage sausage meat
1½ lbs. mushrooms, sliced
½ cup parsley, chopped
sea salt and freshly ground black pepper
wooden skewers

Preheat the oven to 350°F. Rinse the Cornish game hens and season well. Melt the butter in a skillet and sauté the onions until tender. Add the sausage meat, sauté until no longer pink, then add the mushrooms and sauté for 2–3 minutes. Add the parsley and drain off any remaining liquid. Fill each Cornish hen with a cup of stuffing and secure with skewers. Chill until ready to cook. Roast in the preheated oven for 50–60 minutes or until a thermometer inserted into the meat reaches 165°F. Remove the skewers and serve.

Holiday Bavarian Cream

SERVES 8-10

3 tablespoons or envelopes unflavored gelatin
6 egg yolks
1 cup granulated sugar
2 cups milk
1 tablespoon pure vanilla extract
¼ cup brandy or other liqueur of your choice
2 cups whipping cream, whipped
fresh cranberries or other red berries, to garnish
1 large decorative mold

Soak the gelatin in ⅔ cup water for about 5 minutes, or until it has softened and swelled. Whisk the egg yolks in a bowl and gradually add the sugar. Continue to whisk until the mixture is pale yellow. In a saucepan, bring the milk to a full simmer. Remove from the heat and slowly pour into the yolks, whisking constantly. Put the egg and milk in a double boiler. Whisk until the mixture thickens and coats the back of a spoon. Add the gelatin, vanilla, and brandy, and beat well. Put the bowl over a larger bowl of ice water. Stir continuously until the mixture is cool and continues to thicken. Gently fold in the whipped cream using a spatula. Pour into the mold and chill overnight before serving.

A Whimsical New Years Eve

MENU FOR 8-10 GUESTS

APERITIF
Elderflower Champagne Cocktail
With Edible Gold Leaf and Miniature Gardenia Garnish

APPETIZER
Caviar Bar
Caviar of your Choice and Smoked Salmon

A Selection of Trimmings

Served with Wild Rice Blinis, Blini Puffs, and Toast Points

FIRST COURSE
Crab and Lobster Bisque with Sherry
Garnished with Mini Puff Pastry Stars

SECOND COURSE
Ruby Salad
With a Pomegranate Vinaigrette

THIRD COURSE
Miniature Penne with Black Truffle Sage Cream Sauce
With Parmesan Cheese Curls and Fried Sage Leaves

FOURTH COURSE
Lollipop Lamb Chops
With a Pomegranate Wine Sauce and Fresh Mint Relish

FIFTH COURSE
Chocolate Mousse Shooters

Midnight Watch

One of the cardinal rules of New Year's Eve is to have a good time and that is what we kept in mind in designing this wacky assemblage sculpture to keep track of the countdown to midnight at this party. We include plenty of clocks to view from any angle in the room and not let anyone lose track of time. Our intent is to keep things high-spirited and fun, in line with the objective of the party. That means lots of color and lots of movement and we selected the energetic combination of turquoise and coral as a starting point.

This celebration is in the fanciful living room of the former Tony Duquette estate in Beverly Hills, which inspired us to reflect the fantastical designs that he frequently created for the stage and screen in the mid-twentieth century. In the pursuit of an extravagantly theatrical display we wanted a tall piece to make as dramatic a statement as possible—

something in which Duquette specialized. We had fun putting together an unusual pastiche of flowers including eremerus, protea, cock's comb, roses, button mums, freesia, dendrobium orchids, dahlias, and zinnias. We combined them with swirls of conch shells, star fish that we painted turquoise, cascades of clam shells, and a variety of found trinkets and fabric pieces mirroring some of the unusual undersea elements in the house's extraordinary interior.

As a bizarre touch we even painted bronze "hands of time" to reach out from behind the impressive floral sculpture to welcome the guests. Turquoise taper candles highlight this display as well as candelabras placed throughout the party area. A caviar bar stands nearby, capturing the same spirit of decadence, and an exquisite five-course tasting menu is served throughout the long evening.

Elderflower Champagne Cocktail

MAKES 10 DRINKS

10 tablespoons elderflower syrup
2 bottles Champagne, chilled
edible gold leaf
10 miniature white gardenias or rose petals
10 bolla or large wine glasses, chilled

Place 1 tablespoon elderflower syrup in each glass. Top up with chilled Champagne. Sprinkle edible gold leaf on top of each drink and float a miniature gardenia or rose petals to garnish. Serve immediately.

Note: The edible gold leaf is available at Sur La Table or on-line.

Caviar Bar

SERVES 8–10

2–3 varieties of caviar of your choice
    (allow about 2 oz. per person)
½ cup snipped chives
½ cup mild white onion, very finely chopped
1 cup crème fraîche or sour cream
2–3 ripe avocados, peeled, pitted, and chopped
freshly grated zest from 2 unwaxed lemons
½ cup capers in brine, drained
24 wild rice blinis or Blini Puffs (see page 81)
24 toast points (6 slices of toasted bread,
    crusts removed and sliced into fourths)
a selection of prepared unsalted crackers
1 side of smoked salmon, sliced
3–4 fillets of smoked trout
8–10 decorative caviar spoons

Keep the caviar in its tins and find an attractive platter for the smoked fish. Arrange the other ingredients in Martini glasses, Champagne coupes, and glass or silver icers. Fill a large, decorative silver or glass container with plenty of ice. Arrange the caviar and trimmings on top of the ice. Heat the blinis and keep them warm by wrapping them in a starched linen napkin. Be sure to use caviar spoons.

Note: Often, inexpensive caviar spoons are found in second hand stores, Asian markets, or holiday catalogs. At The Kitchen, we pass caviar, crème fraîche, and lemon zest on these spoons as an easy passed appetizer.

Crab and Lobster Bisque with Mini Puff Pastry Stars

SERVES 8-10

¾ cup butter
1 large onion, finely chopped
2 large shallots, minced
⅓ cup all-purpose flour
2 cups half-and-half
2 cups fish, vegetable, or chicken stock
1 cup heavy cream
½ cup dry sherry or white wine
1 teaspoon Tabasco sauce or other hot sauce
1 tablespoon paprika
1 lb. well-cleaned crab meat
½ lb. well-cleaned lobster meat, chopped

Mini Puff Pastry Stars:
1 sheet purchased puff pastry, thawed
¼ cup milk
a small star-shaped cutter
a baking sheet, lightly greased

In a medium stockpot over medium/low heat, melt ½ cup butter and sauté the onion and shallots for 5 minutes. Stir in the flour and cook for another few minutes. Gradually add the half-and-half, fish stock, cream, and sherry and continue cooking until slightly thickened. Season to taste with salt, pepper, Tabasco sauce, and paprika.

Melt the remaining butter in a skillet over medium heat. Add the crab and lobster meat and sauté until heated through. Add to the soup and season to taste. When cool, purée the soup in a blender.

Preheat the oven to 350°F. Lay the puff pastry out on a flat surface. Cut out several stars and place on the prepared baking sheet. Lightly brush with milk. Bake in the preheated oven for 10–12 minutes or until golden. When ready to serve, gently reheat the soup, ladle into serving bowls, and garnish with pastry stars.

Ruby Salad with Pomegranate Vinaigrette

SERVES 8-10

4–5 heads baby red leaf lettuce, torn
2 heads radicchio, cored and torn
3–4 heads red endives, sliced lengthwise
½ cup dried cranberries
½ cup dried cherries
3 red beets, roasted, peeled, and sliced lengthwise
½ cup pomegranate seeds
1 cup candied or toasted pecans
1½ cups crumbled St. Agur (blue cheese)
sea salt and freshly ground black pepper

For the Pomegranate Vinaigrette:
¼ cup pomegranate juice
¼ cup white balsamic vinegar
1 shallot, minced
1 tablespoon chopped mint
1 tablespoon pomegranate molasses
¾ cup canola oil or extra virgin olive oil
sea salt and freshly ground black pepper

To make the Pomegranate Vinaigrette, put the pomegranate juice, vinegar, shallot, mint, and pomegranate molasses in a bowl and whisk to combine. Gradually whisk in the oil. Season to taste with salt and pepper and set aside until needed.

Put the salad greens in a bowl and toss to mix. Add all the remaining salad ingredients. Season with salt and pepper. Add a few tablespoons of the Pomegranate Vinaigrette and toss well. Add a little more, if needed.

Note: Alternatively you could put the dressed salad greens on a platter and arrange the remaining ingredients around the outside edge, to form a garland.

starting with about 1 tablespoon. Season to taste with salt and pepper. Pour the sauce over the pasta and mix. Adjust the seasoning and truffle oil again, if needed. Heat about 2 inches of oil in a large skillet or wok. Fry the sage leaves until crisp and drain on paper towels. Spoon the pasta into bowls and garnish with sage leaves and Parmesan.

Lollipop Lamb Chops
MAKES 24 CHOPS
3 tablespoons each chopped fresh rosemary,
    mint, and basil
olive oil, for brushing
3–8 rib racks of lamb, well trimmed, and frenched
sea salt and freshly ground black pepper
Pomegranate Wine Sauce and Fresh Mint Relish,
    to serve (see below)
a rimmed baking sheet

Put the herbs in a small bowl and mix together. Brush the lamb with oil and season with salt and pepper. Sprinkle the herb mixture over the lamb. Put in the refrigerator and let marinate for an hour or longer.

Preheat the oven to 475°F. Place the racks on a rimmed baking sheet and roast for about 10 minutes or until a meat thermometer inserted into the center reads 130°F. Cut between the bones to make individual chops. Serve with Pomegranate Wine Sauce and Fresh Mint Relish.

POMEGRANATE WINE SAUCE
MAKES 3 CUPS
1 onion, finely chopped
¼ cup butter
2 cups pomegranate juice
1 cup red wine
1 cup beef broth
1 sprig rosemary
¼ cup pomegranate molasses
2 tablespoons cornstarch, dissolved in ¼ cup water
sea salt and freshly ground black pepper

Sauté the onion in a skillet with the butter until softened. Add the pomegranate juice, red wine, beef broth, rosemary, and bring to a boil. Lower the heat and let simmer for several minutes.

Keep the pan over heat and whisk in the cornstarch and water mixture. When the sauce has thickened, add the pomegranate

Miniature Penne with Black Truffle Sage Cream Sauce
SERVES 8-10
1 lb. mini-penne pasta
2 tablespoons unsalted butter
⅓ cup shallots, minced
3 tablespoons sage, chopped
2 cups dry white wine
3 cups heavy cream
black truffle oil, to taste
16–20 sage leaves
corn or vegetable oil, for frying
sea salt and freshly ground black pepper
Parmesan cheese curls, to serve

Bring a large pot of water to a full boil, add a couple dashes of salt, and the pasta. Cook until the pasta is just tender. Drain, rinse, return to the pan, and cover to keep warm.

Melt the butter in a saucepan over medium heat. Add the shallots and sage. Sauté for about 30 seconds. Whisk in the wine and cream. Increase the heat and bring to a soft boil until the sauce is reduced and thickened. Add black truffle oil to taste,

molasses and salt and pepper to taste. Strain the sauce, transfer to a resealable container and refrigerate for up to 2 days. Reheat to serve.

FRESH MINT RELISH
MAKES 1 CUP
1 cup each mint leaves and flatleaf parsley
16 cornichons, cut in half
4 teaspoons capers
½ cup extra virgin olive oil
4 teaspoons white wine vinegar, or to taste
2 tablespoons granulated sugar
sea salt and freshly ground black pepper

Put the mint and parsley leaves in a food processor and blend until finely chopped. Scrape down the sides. Add the cornichons and capers and process to combine. With the motor running, pour the oil down the funnel. Add the vinegar and sugar, and season well with salt and pepper. Transfer to a resealable container and refrigerate until ready to use. The sauce will keep for up to 1 week.

Chocolate Mousse Shooters
MAKES 20 SHOOTERS
8 oz. bittersweet chocolate, roughly chopped
3 tablespoons Kahlúa or liqueur of your choice
1 tablespoon pure vanilla extract
½ cup unsalted butter, cut into cubes
8 large egg yolks
½ cup granulated sugar
5 egg whites
1 cup heavy cream, whipped

Melt the chocolate, liqueur, and vanilla extract in a double boiler, stirring continuously. Remove from the heat and gradually whisk in the butter. Combine the egg yolks and sugar in a mixing bowl and whisk until thick and pale yellow. Slowly add the chocolate mixture and blend well. Beat the egg whites until soft peaks form. Gently fold the egg whites, ¼ at a time, into the chocolate and egg yolk mixture.

Chill until ready to serve. Just before serving, fold in the whipped cream. Spoon into small shot or aperitif glasses to serve.

Chinese New Year

MENU FOR 8–10 GUESTS

APERITIF Lychee Collins

BUFFET Crab Salad Lettuce Cups

Watercress and Mizuni Tropical Fruit Salad
With a Miso Vinaigrette

Stir-Fried Chinese Vegetables

Braised Short Ribs
With Chinese Barbecue Sauce

Shrimp and Corn Fritters

Lobster and Papaya
Served on Sugar Cane Skewers and with Sweet Chili Sauce

DESSERT Individual Pear Tatins

Sesame Seed Tuiles

Fortune Cookies
Dipped in Chocolate and Sprinkled with Gold Dust

Gold Rush

In Chinese tradition, decorating the home on New Year's Day in red and gold brings happiness and wealth. Our grand celebration in the style of Chinese New Year uses gold upon gold upon gold to create a unique and lustrous tabletop that casts a burnished glow and mesmerizes guests into a mood of well-being and celebration. The table linen of gold silk is overlaid with a sheer top decorated with gold appliqué. Gold chargers with gold-rimmed plates and glasses and gold flatware create an exciting and sumptuous look accented by the warmth of gold-leafed votives spread around the table.

Chinese vase stands have been painted gold and stacked high on the table to resemble a pagoda. Broad leaf succulent plants have been painted gold and tucked into its base. Gold-painted bamboo is inserted horizontally and balanced by red lanterns as explosive sprays of yellow oncidium orchids and gold-colored cymbidium orchids spill from the top.

far right As a final touch, red napkins tied with prosperity bracelets rest against traditional individualized name stamps selected for each guest as their place card.

Lychee Collins

MAKES 1 DRINK

2½ fl oz. gin
2 fl oz. freshly squeezed lemon or lime juice
1 fl oz. sugar syrup (see page 73)
1 fl oz. liquid from canned lychee fruit
a splash of club soda
lychee or edible flower, to garnish

Pour the first 4 ingredients into a cocktail shaker filled with ice. Fill a highball glass with crushed ice and strain the drink from the shaker into the glass. Top up with club soda. Garnish and serve immediately.

Crab Salad Lettuce Cups

SERVES 8–10

3 cups cooked lump crabmeat
3 medium tomatoes, peeled, seeded, and chopped
1 cup small cucumbers, chopped
2 tablespoons finely chopped mint
2 tablespoons chopped chives
2 tablespoons chopped cilantro
1 tablespoon lemon zest
¼ cup rice wine vinegar or sherry vinegar
2 tablespoons soy sauce
¾ cup olive or canola oil
iceberg, bibb, or butter lettuce, to serve
cilantro sprigs, to garnish
salt and freshly ground black pepper

Combine the crab, tomatoes, cucumbers, mint, chives, and cilantro in a bowl. In a separate small bowl, mix the lemon zest, rice wine vinegar, and soy sauce. Beat in the olive oil and season to taste with salt and pepper. Prepare lettuce cups using the inner leaves only. To serve, dress the salad with the vinaigrette and fill the lettuce cups. Garnish with cilantro sprigs and serve immediately.

Watercress and Mizuni Tropical Fruit Salad

SERVES 8–10

2 bunches watercress, long stems removed
½ lb. mizuni lettuce
2 tablespoons white miso paste
1 teaspoon prepared wasabi
2 tablespoons rice wine vinegar
⅓ cup canola or olive oil
1 pineapple, peeled, cored, and cut lengthwise into 2–3 inch slices
2 mangos, peeled, pitted, and sliced crosswise into 2–3 inch slices
1 medium jicama, pitted and shredded
sea salt and freshly ground pepper

Put the greens in a salad bowl. In a separate small bowl, combine the miso, wasabi, and rice wine vinegar. Beat in the oil and season to taste with salt and pepper. Pour sufficient vinaigrette over the greens to moisten. Arrange the pineapple, mango, and jicama on top. Serve immediately.

Stir-fried Chinese Vegetables

SERVES 8–10

¼ cup corn or vegetable oil
1 onion, cut into ¼-inch wedges
2 tablespoons grated ginger root
3 garlic cloves, finely minced
1 teaspoon dried hot red pepper flakes
2 red bell peppers, cut into vertical slices
2 yellow bell peppers, cut into vertical slices
½ lb. sugar snaps, trimmed
½ lb. snow peas, trimmed
1 cup frozen edamame, defrosted
1 bunch radish, each one cut in half
6 baby bok choy, each one cut in half
¼ cup bottled spicy Thai sauce

Heat a wok over high heat until a bead of water evaporates on contact. Pour in the oil and reduce the heat to medium. Add the onion and toss until slightly soft. Add the ginger, garlic, red pepper flakes, and bell peppers and toss until the peppers have softened, about 2 minutes. Add the sugar snaps, snow peas, edamame, radish, and baby bok choy and toss until hot, about 3 minutes. Add the spicy Thai sauce, toss and serve immediately.

Braised Short Ribs with Chinese Barbecue Sauce

SERVES 8–10

6 lb. short ribs, boneless
¼ cup oil
6 garlic cloves, peeled and crushed
2 onions, peeled and chopped
2 cups bottled barbecue sauce of your choice
2–3 inch piece ginger root, peeled and grated
salt and freshly ground black pepper

a large roasting pan

Preheat the oven to 450°F. Place the ribs in a large roasting pan with 2 cups water. Season with salt and pepper. Roast in the preheated oven for 25 minutes. Remove the pan from the oven, turn the ribs over and return them to the oven to roast for another 25 minutes. Remove them from the oven a second time and drain any juices, reserve, and set aside. Reduce oven temperature to 375°F. Heat the oil in a skillet and add the garlic and onions. Sauté until softened. Add the reserved meat juices, barbecue sauce, and ginger and heat through. Pour the sauce over the ribs, cover with foil, and roast for about 2 hours or until the ribs are tender.

to check seasoning and consistency. Add salt and pepper if necessary and if the batter is too thin, add a few tablespoons of flour. Working in batches, drop tablespoons of batter into the oil and fry each until golden brown. Remove from the pan with a slotted spoon and drain on paper towels. Serve immediately.

Lobster and Papaya on Sugar Cane Skewers

MAKES 24-30 SKEWERS
2 x 8–10 oz. lobster tails, cooked
1–2 papayas and/or mangos, peeled and pitted
   bottled Thai sweet chili sauce, to serve
24–30 sugar cane sticks or bamboo skewers

Clean and slice lobster tails into ¼-inch thick slices. Thinly slice the papaya, or mangos lengthwise. Weave a slice of papaya and alternate on a sugar cane stick with cooked lobster slices. Chill and brush with Thai sweet chili sauce before serving.

Individual Pear Tatins

SERVES 8-10
1½ cups sugar
½ cup water
2 tablespoons pear liqueur or Grand Marnier
8–10 pears (comice or Asian)
8 oz. butter, melted
1 lb. purchased puff pastry, thawed if frozen
8–10 ramekins or foil cups

Preheat the oven to 375°F. Combine the sugar, water, and liqueur in a saucepan. Heat until the mixture caramelizes. Pour some of the caramel sauce into ramekins or foil cups. Let rest while you peel and core the pears. Trim them by cutting off the top and the bottom so that sit in the ramekins without wobbling. Brush with melted butter, and place each one in a ramekin. Place on a baking sheet and bake in the preheated oven for 30–35 minutes, until just tender.

Roll out the puff pastry on a lightly-floured surface and cut into circles to fit the ramekins. Remove the pears from the oven and place a puff pastry round on top of each ramekin. Return to the oven and bake for another 20–25 minutes or until the fruit is soft and the puff pastry browned. When cool

Shrimp and Corn Fritters

MAKES 12-36 FRITTERS
¾ cup all-purpose flour
½ teaspoon baking powder
½ teaspoon salt
1 large egg, beaten
3 tablespoons coconut milk or milk
1 teaspoon grated ginger root
1 teaspoon hot sauce or dried hot red pepper flakes
1½ cups fresh corn kernels
½ cup raw shrimp, finely chopped
⅓ cup green onion, chopped
  canola or vegetable oil for frying
  sea salt and freshly ground black pepper

Sift together the flour, baking powder, and salt. Put the egg, coconut milk, ginger, and hot sauce in a bowl and mix. Add the flour mixture and stir until just combined. Add the corn kernels, shrimp, and green onion and gently stir to mix.

When ready to serve, heat 2 inches of oil in a wok or deep fryer. Drop 1 tablespoon of batter into the oil and fry until golden. Taste

enough to handle carefully turn the tatins out onto serving plates and drizzle with the remaining caramel sauce. Serve immediately, or reheat before serving.

Sesame Seed Tuiles

MAKES 12 LARGE OR 24 SMALL TUILES
1½ cups confectioners' sugar
½ cup butter, softened
¾ cup toasted sesame seeds
½ all-purpose or cake flour
½ cup freshly squeezed orange juice or milk
1 tablespoon finely grated orange peel
a baking sheet, greased and lined with
   parchment paper or a silicone baking mat

Preheat oven to 325°F. Combine all the ingredients in a mixer bowl and beat well.

Place 1 tablespoon batter for a small tuile or 2 tablespoons batter for a large tuile, on the prepared baking sheet. Spread out very thinly using a spatula. Bake in the preheated oven for 5–8 minutes or until golden. Working quickly, lift the tuiles one at a time and roll them around a narrow rolling pin or wood dowel. Slide off the tip of the rolling pin and place on a plate to cool. If the tuile hardens before you roll it, return to the oven for 1 minute to soften.

Store the tuiles in a large airtight container and use within 1 week of making.

Chocolate and Gold Fortune Cookies

MAKES 16 COOKIES
16 purchased Chinese fortune cookies
5 oz. semisweet chocolate
  edible gold dust, to decorate

Melt the chocolate in a metal bowl over simmering water, being careful not to scorch it. Stir with a rubber spatula until completely melted and smooth.

Let the chocolate cool slightly then, holding a cookie firmly between your thumb and index finger, dip the bottom of it half way into the melted chocolate. Lay on a sheet of parchment and repeat with the remaining cookies. Sprinkle with gold dust before the chocolate sets. Store in an airtight container and use within 2 weeks of making.

Mexican Fiesta Nueva

MENU FOR 6–8 GUESTS

APERITIF Pomegranate Margarita

TO BE PASSED Corn Fritters

With Roasted Tomato Sauce

Miniature Chile Rellenos

With Chipotle Sauce

BUFFET Build Your Own Tostada

"Fan Shell" Corn Tostada Shells

Grilled Steak, Chicken Breast, and Cooked Jumbo Shrimp

Grated Monterey Jack and Cheddar Cheeses

Shredded Iceberg Lettuce, Green Onions, Tomatoes, and Sliced Avocado

Chipotle Peppers, Olives, Pico de Gallo, and Papaya and Pineapple Salsas

Sour Cream and Guacamole

Mexican Red Rice

Chicken Enchiladas

With Cheese Sauce

Fire and Ice Salad

DESSERT Kahlùa Chocolate Crêpes

With Hot Fudge Sauce

above Small clay pots of mini sunflowers hang from the limbs of an old California melaleuca tree behind an updated version of a Mexican buffet.

"*Mark's Garden is one of the most elegant and exquisite florists I have ever used. Consistently over the top, always more than you could expect. The designers are so wonderfully talented with their use of color and style that they actually seem to breathe life into their arrangements. Without exception, always stunning, and perfect for that special occasion. In short, Mark's Garden delivers... in more ways than one!*"

Larry King

Southwest Chic

A contemporary California style is the approach we chose to present this very traditional Mexican menu. With a classic California-style Spanish patio as the setting, we have set out casual tables under umbrellas and taken our color cues from the natural earth tones of the American southwest. Beige and terracotta tones are mixed with the muted green hues of local succulent plants and mosses. Hopsack linens with simple pottery dishes complemented by crisp linen napkins lend an unexpected fresh, modern look.

A mixture of succulent plants in dusky shades of green and red are gathered in a shallow clay bowl forming a miniature cactus garden as the centerpiece for this casual table. Twigs, branches, and wood bark are combined as "floral" elements to add some architectural structure to the piece. Small hand-blown shot glasses holding tiny cacti are added near each plate to unite the place settings with the centerpiece and offer a lovely take-home favor for each guest. Instead of a traditional piñata, small distressed clay pots sprouting mini-sunflowers and yellow daisies are strung from the ribs of the umbrellas to dangle fancifully overhead.

Pomegranate Margarita

MAKES 1 DRINK

2 fl oz. tequila
1 fl oz. pomegranate juice
¾ fl oz. freshly squeezed lemon or lime juice
pomegranate seeds, to garnish (optional)

Pour all of the ingredients into a glass tumbler filled with ice. Garnish with pomegranate seeds and serve immediately.

Miniature Chile Rellenos with Chipotle Sauce

MAKES 18-24

8 oz. jack cheese, cut into ½-inch cubes
8 canned green chiles, cut into strips
4 eggs, separated
¼ teaspoon salt
2 tablespoons all-purpose flour
vegetable oil, for deep frying
toothpicks, to serve

Heat the oil in a wok until very hot. Wrap the cheese cubes with a green chile strip and secure with a toothpick. Beat the egg whites until very stiff. Beat the egg yolks well with 1 teaspoon water and salt and fold them into the whites. Fold in the flour. Dip each chile cheese cube into the batter, making sure each one is well covered. Gently slide into the hot oil and fry until golden brown, turning to cook both sides. Do not crowd the wok. Remove with a slotted spoon and drain on paper towels. Serve hot with Chipotle Sauce.

CHIPOTLE SAUCE

MAKES 1¼ CUPs

¾ cup good-quality mayonnaise
½ cup sour cream
2 tablespoons chipotle chiles in adobo sauce, finely chopped
sea salt and freshly ground black pepper

Put the ingredients in a medium bowl and stir to combine. Season to taste with salt and pepper. Will keep for 2–3 days if refrigerated in an airtight container

Corn Fritters with Roasted Tomato Sauce

MAKES 20-30 APPETIZERS

2 cups whole corn kernels (either cut fresh from the cob or frozen, do not use canned)
1 egg, lightly beaten
⅓ cup finely chopped scallions, white part only
¼ teaspoon finely minced garlic
2 tablespoons finely chopped cilantro
¼ cup finely chopped white onion
½ cup all-purpose flour
¼ cup cornmeal
½ teaspoon salt
½ teaspoon baking powder
½ teaspoon ground coriander
corn oil, for frying

Heat the oil in a wok until very hot. Mix all of the ingredients together. Using two spoons or your fingers, drop small dollops into the oil and fry until golden brown. Remove with a slotted spoon and drain on paper towels. Serve warm with Roasted Tomato Sauce

ROASTED TOMATO SAUCE

MAKES 3 CUPS

½ white onion, coarsely chopped
3-4 garlic cloves
6-8 ripe red tomatoes, sliced in half
1 teaspoon smoked Spanish paprika (pimentón)
olive oil, to drizzle
chicken stock, to thin when blending
a handful of basil or parsley, chopped (optional)
freshly squeezed lemon juice (optional)
sea salt and freshly ground black pepper
a non-stick sheet pan

Preheat the oven to 375°F. Toss the onion, garlic, tomatoes, paprika, and olive oil in bowl. Spread on a sheet pan and bake in the preheated oven until slightly caramelized and soft.

Purée the tomato mixture in a blender and add chicken stock slowly until the sauce is the desired consistency. Season to taste with salt and pepper. Stir in the herbs and a dash of lemon juice, if using.

Mexican Red Rice

SERVES 8-10

2 cups long grain rice
½ cup vegetable oil
¾ cup tomato paste
4 cups boiling water
1 teaspoon salt
½ teaspoon freshly ground black pepper

Several hours before serving, put the rice in hot water and let stand for 2–3 hours. Drain the water and allow the rice to dry on paper towels for about 1 hour.

Put the oil in a large pot, add the rice, and fry until it is browned. Drain any excess oil. Add the tomato paste and simmer for 5 minutes over low heat, stirring constantly. Stir in the boiling water and season with salt and pepper. Cover and let cook over low heat for about 30 minutes, stirring occasionally, or until the rice is tender and all the water has been absorbed.

Chicken Enchiladas with Cheese Sauce

SERVES 8-10

For the filling:

3 large yellow onions, chopped

3 tablespoons oil or butter

6 poached chicken breasts, pulled into strips

12 oz. canned green chiles, chopped

3 cups shredded jack cheese (reserve 1 cup for topping enchiladas)

10-12 corn tortillas, warmed to soften

3 tablespoons oil

For the cheese sauce:

¾ cup butter

½ cup all-purpose flour

1½ teaspoons salt

1½ teaspoons white pepper

2 cups milk

1½ cups chicken stock

1½ cups sour cream

2 cups shredded jack cheese

To serve:

1½ cups bottled green chili salsa

3 medium tomatoes, chopped

1 avocado, sliced

a few sprigs of cilantro

lime wedges, to serve

a large, rectangular baking dish, oiled

To make the cheese sauce, melt the butter in a saucepan, add the flour, and stir until a light brown. Add the salt, pepper, milk, and chicken stock. Cook until thickened. Add the sour cream and cheese. Season to taste.

Preheat the oven to 375°F. Sauté the onion in oil until lightly browned. Add the pulled chicken, green chiles and 2 cups of jack cheese. Lay the tortillas flat and fill each one with about ½ cup of filling. Roll the tortillas and arrange in lines in the prepared dish. Pour cheese sauce over the top. Bake in the preheated oven for about 20 minutes or until lightly browned. Remove from the oven, sprinkle with the remaining jack cheese and return to the oven for 5 more minutes, or until the cheese has melted. Garnish with green chili salsa, tomatoes, avocado, cilantro, and lime wedges to serve.

Fire and Ice Salad

SERVES 8-10

1 cup dark brown sugar

3 cups water

1 tablespoon dried hot red pepper flakes

¼ cup freshly squeezed lemon juice

2 mangos, peeled, pitted, and cut into chunks

2 papayas, peeled, seeded, and cut into chunks

1 pineapple, peeled, cored, and cut into chunks

6 Persian cucumbers, sliced

1 cantaloupe, peeled, seeded and cut into chunks

1 honeydew, peeled, seeded and cut into chunks

½ cup chopped basil

½ cup chopped mint

6 handfuls of watercress, washed

Put the sugar and water in a saucepan and simmer until the sugar has dissolved. Remove from the heat and add the red pepper flakes and lemon juice.

Combine all the other ingredients, except the watercress, in a large salad bowl. Pour the sugar mixture over the fruit and toss to coat. Lay a bed of watercress on a platter and top with the fruit. Serve immediately.

Kahlúa Chocolate Crêpes

SERVES 8-10

8 oz. semisweet chocolate, cut into chunks

1½ cups heavy whipping cream

½ cup Kahlúa, or to taste

whipped cream, to serve

bittersweet chocolate shavings, to garnish

Hot Fudge Sauce (see page 74), to serve (optional)

For the crêpe batter:

1 cup all-purpose flour

1 tablespoon sugar

¼ teaspoon salt

3 eggs, lightly beaten

1 cup milk

⅓ cup water

3 tablespoons melted unsalted butter

unsalted butter, for frying

a piping bag or gallon-size zip-lock bag

First make the mousse. In a double boiler, slowly melt the semisweet chocolate. Be careful not to scorch with too high a heat. Once melted, remove from the heat and allow to cool, stirring occasionally. In a separate large, high sided bowl, whip the heavy cream and Kahlúa until medium peaks form. Pour in ⅓ of the chocolate at a time and continue to whip to stiff peaks, being careful not to overbeat. Chill until needed.

To make the batter, sift the flour, sugar, and salt into a large bowl. In a separate bowl, whisk the eggs, then add the milk, water, and butter. Mix well. Add to the dry ingredients and combine until smooth. Cover with plastic wrap and let the batter rest at room temperature for one hour. Heat a crêpe or omelet pan. Melt a little butter and swirl it round the pan to coat. Pour a little batter into the pan and swirl it around to make a thin film by quickly rotating and tilting the pan. When the underside is golden brown, flip with a spatula. Cook the other side for only a few seconds, it does not need to be brown. Stack the crêpes on a plate and cover with foil to keep warm.

To assemble, fill a pastry bag or zip-lock bag with the chocolate mousse. If using a zip-lock bag, cut the tip diagonally. Lay the crêpes on a flat surface and pipe a thick line of mousse down the center. Fold the crêpes. Serve with whipped cream and Hot Fudge Sauce. Garnish with chocolate shavings.

A Rustic Italian Dinner

MENU FOR 6-8 GUESTS

APERITIF   Blood Orange Prosecco

TO BE PASSED   Fried Sage Leaves
With Italian Sausage and Parmesan Cheese Filling

BUFFET   Antipasti Platter
A Selection of Italian Cheeses to include Gorgonzola and Soft Goat Cheese

A Variety of Salami and Meats to include Soppressata, Bresaola, and Prosciutto

Marinated Artichoke Hearts, Marinated Olives, Cerignola Olives, Roasted Red

and Golden Beets, Grilled Red and Yellow Bell Peppers, and Fresh Figs

Served with a Basket of Breadsticks and Seeded Cracker Breads

Sautéed Big Shrimp with Orange "Dust"
Served on a Bed of Lemon, Orange, and Lime Wheels

Turkey Breast with Pancetta
And White Wine Sauce

DESSERT   Grand Marnier Chocolate Stuffed Figs

Sgroppino

above left A compote of kumquats and fresh herb topiaries accent the table décor.

above right A hollowed artichoke makes a unique and attractive vase for orange ranunculus.

"Mark's Garden exhibits an artistry that I have rarely seen by another florist. They are capable of producing extravagant and magnificent floral designs that transform a room and evoke a spirit of their own. They can also create precious one-of-a-kind objets d'art incorporating natural and unexpected materials that are a joy to behold. They have provided many gorgeous creations for my family over the years and we are always thrilled with their work. In the world of design there is nothing else like them."

Oscar de la Renta

Benvenuto!

The mention of an Italian dinner conjures images of a warm, convivial group gathered for a good time and that was exactly the sense we had going into this. We selected a beautiful rustic setting and bright earthy tones of deep reds, terracotta, rust, and orange to capture the mood and spirit of this party. We know there is to be a lot of great food so we set a large table with a relaxed and casual feel, inviting our guests to sit and talk and eat as long as they want.

Red and terracotta roses, yellow-tipped orange tulips and orange ranunculus in vintage clay pots share the table with herb topiaries, moss, and bowls of kumquats to provide an authentic feel without resorting to the expected standby for Italian décor like sunflowers or daisies. In our usual pursuit of something new, we also decided to use linen panels interwoven across the table rather than a standard tablecloth. These panels are handy to have because they can be used in so many different ways. The buffet table is a cascade of roses flowing from a wire pillar on to the table and surrounding the food. For a whimsical touch, we covered a bench with moss and ferns of varying shades of green, more as a unique décor touch than for seating.

Blood Orange Prosecco
MAKES 8 DRINKS

1½ cups blood orange juice, strained and chilled
1 x 750-ml bottle of Prosecco or sparkling wine, well chilled
8 thin slices of blood orange, to garnish (optional)
8 Champagne flutes or similar, well chilled

Pour 3 tablespoons blood orange juice into a chilled Champagne flute. Slowly pour in the chilled Prosecco.

Garnish each glass with a slice of blood orange, if using. Serve immediately.

Fried Sage Leaves with Italian Sausage and Parmesan Cheese Filling

MAKES 25 APPETIZERS

48 sage leaves
¼ lb. Parmesan cheese, finely grated
½ lb. Italian sausage meat
2 eggs, beaten
2 cups panko bread crumbs
light vegetable oil, for deep frying

Wash the sage leaves and pat dry. Heat the oil in a wok or large pot until very hot. Top a sage leaf with 1 teaspoon Parmesan cheese and 1–2 teaspoons Italian sausage. Press another sage leaf on top of the cheese and sausage. Dip each sage leaf in the egg and roll in bread crumbs. Deep fry until golden brown and the sausage is cooked. Serve with Roasted Tomato Sauce (see page 105) but omit the pimentón from the recipe.

Sautéed Big Shrimp with Orange "Dust"

SERVES 8–10

3 oranges, plus 2 for garnish
3 lemons, plus 2 for garnish
3 limes, plus 2 for garnish
2 tablespoons paprika
2 tablespoons onion powder
1 tablespoon sea salt
1 tablespoon shallots, minced
3 tablespoons vegetable oil
3 tablespoons butter
24–32 large raw shrimp, shells and veins removed, tails on
salt and freshly ground black pepper

Grate the peel from the oranges, lemons, and limes. Save the flesh and squeeze the juice into a separate container. Set aside. Mix the grated peel with the paprika, onion powder, and salt. Spread the peel mixture onto a baking sheet, and let dry at room temperature for 3–4 hours or overnight. Sauté the shallots in oil and butter over medium heat until soft. Add the shrimp, half of the peel mixture, and reserved citrus juice. Continue to sauté until the shrimp is opaque. Season to taste with salt and pepper. Slice the remaining citrus fruit to garnish and arrange on the bottom of a large platter. Top with the cooked shrimp and sprinkle with additional peel mixture to taste.

Antipasti Platter

SERVES 8

8–10 oz. Gorgonzola
8–10 oz. soft goat cheese
12–16 slices bresaola
12–16 slices soppressata salami
12–16 slices prosciutto
2 red bell peppers, roasted, skin removed, seeded, and sliced
2 yellow bell peppers, roasted, skin removed, seeded, and sliced
12 oz. marinated artichoke hearts
12 oz. marinated olives and/or cerignola olives
1 large golden beet, roasted, peeled, and diced
1 large red beet, roasted, peeled, and diced
2–3 fresh figs, quartered
a handful of basil leaves
1 bunch flatleaf parsley, chopped
olive oil, to drizzle
Italian breadsticks and seeded cracker bread, to serve

Arrange all the ingredients on a large platter and garnish with basil leaves and parsley. Drizzle with olive oil. Serve with a basket of Italian breadsticks (grissini) and seeded cracker bread.

Turkey Breast with Pancetta and White Wine Sauce

SERVES 8-10

1 (4-5 lbs.) boneless turkey breast
½ lb. pancetta or bacon
¼ cup chopped parsley
½ cup chopped basil
1 tablespoon sea salt
1 tablespoon cracked black pepper
8–10 lengths of butcher's twine or string

Preheat the oven to 325°F. Pound the turkey breast to flatten slightly. Layer the pancetta, parsley, basil, salt, and pepper on top. Roll the turkey breast lengthwise and tie with butcher's twine.

Place in a roasting pan and in the preheated oven to cook for about 3 hours or until a thermometer inserted into the meat reads 160°F. Remove from the oven and allow to rest for 5 minutes. Slice and serve with White Wine Sauce.

WHITE WINE SAUCE

MAKES APPROXIMATELY 2 CUPS

⅓ cup unsalted butter
⅓ cup all-purpose flour
2 cups white wine
2 cups chicken stock
2 tablespoons white balsamic vinegar
2 tablespoons freshly squeezed lemon juice
4 shallots, finely chopped
1 teaspoon each of finely chopped thyme, rosemary, and sage
sea salt and freshly ground black pepper

In a large sauté pan over medium heat, melt the butter and whisk in the flour to make a light brown roux.

In a separate heavy, large sauté pan, bring the white wine, chicken stock, white balsamic vinegar, lemon juice, and shallots to a boil. Reduce the heat, add the chopped herbs and allow to simmer until reduced by half. Slowly whisk in the roux to create the desired consistency. Season to taste with salt and pepper and serve while still hot.

Grand Marnier Chocolate Stuffed Figs

MAKES 24-36 FIGS

1 cup heavy cream
8 oz. semisweet chocolate, finely chopped
2 tablespoons Grand Marnier
24-36 fresh figs
1½ lbs. semisweet chocolate
a pastry bag fitted with a small round tip

Heat the cream in a saucepan over medium/high heat until it just begins to boil. Remove from the heat and add the 8 oz. chocolate and Grand Marnier. Stir until smooth and pour the mixture into a bowl, cover with plastic wrap (so that it touches the top of the chocolate) and let set for 6-8 hours at room temperature.

Use a skewer to enlarge the hole in the bottom of each fig. When the ganache is set, gently stir it with a plastic spatula to loosen. Transfer to a pastry bag fitted with a small round tip. Pipe each fig full of the mixture. Chill for at least an hour.

In a double boiler, gently melt the remaining chocolate and let cool, stirring occasionally. Dip the bottom half of the figs in the melted chocolate and place on a parchment-lined baking sheet. Let set at room temperature. Serve within a few hours of making.

Sgroppino

SERVES 8-10

3 cups heavy whipping cream
½ cup freshly squeezed lemon juice
1½ cups sugar
3 tablespoons finely grated lemon zest
1 bottle Prosecco or other sparkling white wine (750 ml), well chilled
candied lemon peel and/or mint sprigs, to garnish

In a large bowl, mix the cream, lemon juice, sugar, and lemon zest until blended. Pour into a shallow dish, cover, and freeze overnight or for several days.

Before serving, take the lemon ice cream out of the freezer to soften. Transfer to a large bowl and roughly mash or break up with a whisk. Gradually whisk in the Prosecco to your preferred thickness. Spoon into a Martini glass, garnish as desired, and serve

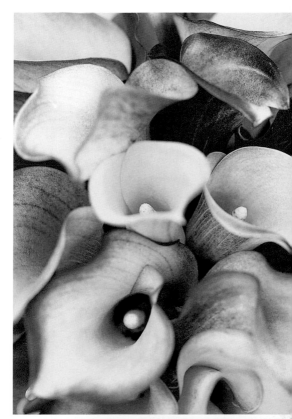

A Green Tea

MENU FOR 8-10

TO DRINK	Frozen Kiwi Daiquiri
	A Selection of Fine Teas
TO BE PASSED	Crab Salad on Brioche Toast
	With Wasabi Caviar
	Belgian Endive with Chèvre
SAVORY TABLE	Open Face Tea Sandwiches
	Cucumber Curls, Cilantro Chutney, and Herbed Cream Cheese
	Crab with Red Pepper Chutney
	Cocktail Shrimp and Fresh Dill
	Closed Face Tea Sandwiches
	Rare Roast Beef with Watercress and Horseradish Sauce
	Chicken Salad with Tarragon
	Deviled Egg with Fresh Dill
	Tomato and Cucumber with Herbed Cream Cheese
	Ham and Baby Greens with Honey Mustard
SWEET TABLE	Warm Anne Boleyn Tarts
	Meringue Kisses with Kiwi Fruit Fool
	Coconut Cake
	With Lemon Curd and Whipped Vanilla Cream

Mother Nature Rules

Here is a tea party to raise awareness and pay tribute to the natural environment. With this all-green theme we demonstrate the beauty and splendor of nature, embracing within our décor many plants and wildlife ranging from the tropical rainforests, to the jungles and the plains of Africa. Combining species of green flora from all around the world we remind ourselves of the precious nature of our own being as well as that of all the things on the planet.

A majestic handmade tree of willow branches sweeps upward from the center of the table, merging a dense growth of vines, ferns, and moss with exotic orchids, tropical anthurium, and venus flytraps. Our table is covered with a natural green silk linen over a skirt of real magnolia leaves and set with Hermès' delicate "Africa" pattern china featuring wild animals. At every place setting a tiny seedling tree in a tied burlap bag is presented to each guest to take home for planting. In the background we have filled large shells mounted on the walls with gracefully draping amaranthus and dendrobium orchids. The buffet display is a mixture of poppy pods, green calla lilies, green zinnia, green anthurium, and mixed exotic ferns.

Frozen Kiwi Daiquiri

MAKES 20 DRINKS

12 oz. can frozen lemonade concentrate, thawed
6 oz. can frozen limeade concentrate, thawed
1 bottle light rum (750 ml)
2–3 cups kiwi purée
lime or kiwi slices, to garnish

Combine all the ingredients, except the kiwi purée, with 4 cups water in a large container and freeze for 24 hours. When ready to serve, remove from the freezer and break up with a spoon. Add kiwi purée to taste and stir. Serve in your choice of well-chilled glass, garnished as desired.

Crab Salad on Brioche Toast

MAKES 18-20 APPETIZERS

1 teaspoon grated lemon zest
2 tablespoons freshly squeezed lemon juice
3 tablespoons extra virgin olive oil
1 lb. lump crabmeat, picked over for cartilage
¼ cup thinly sliced scallions
1–2 tablespoons good-quality mayonnaise (optional)
4 oz. wasabi caviar
salt and freshly ground black pepper

In a bowl, combine the lemon zest, lemon juice, and olive oil. Season with salt and pepper. Add the crab and scallions and mix to combine. Add a small amount of mayonnaise to bind the mixture, if desired. Cover and refrigerate.

To serve, pile a couple of teaspoons of crab salad on top of each Brioche Toast. Finish with wasabi caviar.

BRIOCHE TOASTS

MAKES 50-60 TOASTS

1 loaf Brioche bread, crusts removed, cut into
    ½ inch slices and each slice quartered
½ cup butter, melted

Preheat the oven to 400°F. Brush both sides of the bread with butter. Place on a baking sheet and cook for 5–10 minutes or until brown and crisp. Keep the leftovers in an airtight container for up to 1 week.

Tea Sandwiches

Tasty little tea sandwiches are a snap to make. Use your favorite bakery's bread and ask if they will slice the bread vertically. A variety of breads and fillings is appealing and adds interest to a tea table.

Flavor softened butter with herbs, curry paste, hot sauce, horseradish, or other savory choices. Prepare several fillings such as chicken and chutney, egg salad, deviled ham, crab or shrimp salad, and thinly sliced roast beef, ham, turkey, lamb, pork, cheeses, tomatoes, and cucumbers.

Remove the crusts from the bread. Spread all the slices with softened butter and spread your sandwich filling on half the slices. Top with the remaining bread slices. Cut the sandwiches into squares, rectangles, or triangles, or even make cut-out novelty shapes with cookie cutters.

If you like, butter some of the sandwich edges with softened butter and dip in toasted nuts or chopped herbs. Sandwiches can be made several hours ahead of time. To keep them moist, cover with paper towels, spray lightly with water, and cover with plastic wrap.

Belgian Endive with Chèvre

MAKES 36 APPETIZERS

2 x 5½ oz. logs chèvre, at room temperature
1 cup cream cheese, at room temperature
½ teaspoon Tabasco or other hot sauce
1½ lb. package frozen roasted tomatoes, thawed,
    or 12 oz. bottled sun-dried tomatoes
½ lb. (4–5 heads) Belgian endive, leaves separated,
    rinsed, and chilled
1 bunch chives, cut into 1-inch lengths

Combine the chèvre, cream cheese, and
Tabasco. Chop the tomatoes. Add any
tomato marinade to the cheese and mix.
Put 1 tablespoon cheese mixture on each
leaf and garnish with chopped tomatoes
and chives. Refrigerate until ready to serve.

Warm Anne Boleyn Tarts

MAKES 24 TARTS

2 sheets frozen puff pastry, thawed and rolled
¼ cup cottage cheese
3 tablespoons butter, softened
2 eggs, beaten
3 tablespoons brandy
½ cup granulated sugar
¼ cup mashed potato (instant is suitable)
¼ cup almonds, toasted and ground
grated zest of 2 unwaxed lemons
½ teaspoon nutmeg
3 tablespoons freshly squeezed lemon juice
confectioners' sugar or lemon glaze, for topping
2 x 12-cup mini-muffin pans, buttered
a small cookie cutter

Preheat the oven to 350°F. Cut out 24 small
rounds of pastry and press them down into
the cups in the prepared muffin pans. In a
mixer, beat the cottage cheese and butter
together. Add the eggs, brandy, and sugar
and mix well. In a separate bowl, beat
together the potato, almonds, lemon zest,
nutmeg, and lemon juice. Gradually blend
in the cheese mixture. Beat thoroughly.
Spoon the filling into the pastry shells and
bake for 25–30 minutes or until set. Sift
confectioners' sugar over the tarts, or mix
together sugar and lemon juice to make a
glaze to drizzle over the top. Serve warm.

Meringue Kisses with Kiwi Fruit Fool

MAKES 30–35

8 large egg whites
¾ teaspoon salt
2 cups granulated sugar
a pastry bag fitted with a plain tip
2 baking sheets lined with parchment paper

KIWI FRUIT FOOL

1 cup heavy cream
¾ cup confectioners' sugar
½ cup sour cream or crème fraîche
¾ cup mashed kiwi fruit

Preheat the oven to 175°F or lowest setting.

Beat the egg whites and salt in a mixer on
high speed until they just hold stiff peaks.
Gradually add the sugar. Continue to beat
on high until the whites hold stiff, glossy
peaks. Spoon into the pastry bag and pipe
1-inch kisses onto the prepared baking
sheets. Bake until dry, about 2 hours.

To make the fool, beat the heavy cream in
a mixer until soft peaks form. Gradually add
the sugar and beat until stiff peaks hold.
Gently fold in the sour cream and mashed
kiwi fruit. Serve the Meringue Kisses with
the Kiwi Fruit Fool as a dip.

Coconut Cake

MAKES A 9-INCH ROUND CAKE

1½ sticks unsalted butter, room temperature
1½ cups sugar
2 cups all-purpose or cake flour
2 teaspoons baking powder
¼ teaspoon salt
3 large eggs plus 1 yolk
¾ cup milk
3 teaspoons pure vanilla extract
lemon curd (see right) and whipped
    vanilla cream (see right)
coconut flakes, to fill and decorate
2 x 9-inch round cake pans, buttered and
lined with parchment paper

Preheat the oven to 350°F. In a large bowl,
beat the butter and sugar until light and
fluffy. In a separate bowl, sift and mix the
flour, baking powder, and salt. In a third
bowl, combine all the eggs, milk, and vanilla
extract. Add a third of the flour mixture to the
butter mixture, then add half the milk mixture.
Repeat, ending with the last third of flour
mixture, scraping down the bowl often.

Pour into the prepared pans and bake for
25–30 minutes, or until the center springs
back when lightly pressed. Let cool in the
pans for 5 minutes, then turn out on to a
wire rack and let cool completely.

Trim the sides and top of each cake to make
even. Top one cake with lemon curd, add
whipped cream and coconut, and put the
second cake on top. Frost with whipped
cream and decorate all over with coconut.

LEMON CURD

MAKES 3½ CUPS

8 egg yolks
1½ cups sugar
zest and freshly squeezed juice of 6 unwaxed
lemons, plus extra juice to make ½ cup, if needed
1½ sticks butter, cold and cut into cubes

Bring a couple inches of water to a simmer
in a pan. In a metal bowl, whisk together the
egg yolks, sugar, lemon juice, and zest until
smooth. Put over the simmering water and
continue to whisk until thick and light yellow,
about 10 minutes. Remove from heat and
whisk in the butter, 2 cubes at a time.
When the butter is completely incorporated,
transfer to a container, and cover the surface
of the curd with a layer of plastic wrap.
Refrigerate overnight and up to 2 weeks.

WHIPPED VANILLA CREAM

3 cups heavy whipping cream
2 tablespoons pure vanilla extract
1 cup confectioners' sugar

In a mixing bowl, whip the cream and vanilla
to soft peaks. Gradually add the sugar and
whip to stiff peaks. Refrigerate until needed.

California Wine Tasting

MENU FOR 6–8 GUESTS

TO DRINK	A Tasting of Wine from the Henry Wine Group
TO BE SET OUT	Blue Cheese Terrine

With Roasted Grapes and Rosemary Cashew Nuts

Smoked Salmon and Provolone Loaf

With Dill and Capers

Crab Mousse

Panini in Paper

Pesto Chicken, Brie and Prosciutto, Smoked Salmon and Cream Cheese

Carol Henry's Shrimp

With Ginger and Herb Butter

"The Kitchen's" Cheese Toast

Fine Wines

right We employ robust jewel tone colors and shades of green to tie into the beautiful natural surroundings and, of course, bunches of grapes that we incorporate into the décor.

When we think of wine today we not only imagine French and Italian countrysides but our own Napa Valley where some of the finest wines in the world are now grown. When we found this location in our own "backyard" we immediately recognized what a perfect setting it would be for our wine tasting party. We wanted it to be casual but elegant to reflect the sophisticated wines and menu we planned, so we have set up a table under a soaring oak tree. Large buffet arrangements burst with deep red and hot orange roses mixed with red Gloriosa lilies, purple scabiosa and alium, red dahlias, orange tulips, and green viburnum. The arrangements and the table are draped with cascades of red and green grapes and the tapestry-covered table is entwined with live grape vines, ivy, and moss. The floral highlights, however, are the deep red rose "glamellias" mounted on Tag Anderson-designed metal flutes rising above the table. Glamellias are wonderfully oversized blooms handmade from individually applied rose petals attached to a foam base. They are a Mark's Garden signature design.

Panini in Paper

EACH RECIPE MAKES 8–10 PANINI
You will need a panini press, waxed
paper, and twine.

Pesto Chicken:
3 cloves garlic
¾ cup pine nuts
1 cup Parmesan cheese, grated
3 cups loosely packed basil
⅔ cup extra virgin olive oil, plus extra for brushing
sea salt and freshly ground black pepper
3 chicken breasts, cooked, cooled, and shredded
1 cup baby arugula
1 loaf ciabatta bread, sliced in half lengthwise

To make the pesto, put the garlic in a food
processor and pulse to a fine chop. Add
½ cup pine nuts, ⅔ cup cheese, the basil,
1 teaspoon salt, ½ teaspoon pepper, and
process until finely chopped. With the motor
running, add the oil in a slow and steady
stream, blending until well combined.
Adjust seasoning if necessary. Combine the
shredded chicken, pesto, and remaining
cheese and pine nuts in a bowl. Season to
taste and add the arugula.

Heat the panini press. Spread the chicken
mixture on the bread, close, and brush both
sides with olive oil. Cook in the press for
3–4 minutes, until the crust is golden
and crispy. Cut into bite-size squares or
rectangles. Wrap with paper and tie with
twine. Serve warm.

Brie and Prosciutto:
¼ cup good-quality mayonnaise
1 loaf ciabatta bread, sliced in half lengthwise
½ lb. brie, cut into slices
½ small red onion, thinly sliced
¼ lb. prosciutto, very thinly sliced
olive oil, for brushing

Heat the panini press. Spread mayonnaise
on both cut sides of the bread and arrange
the brie, onion, and prosciutto on one side.
Close and brush with olive oil.

Cook in the panini press for 3–4 minutes,
until the crust is golden and crispy. Cut into
bite-size squares or rectangles. Wrap with
paper and tie with twine. Serve warm.

Smoked Salmon and Cream Cheese:
½ cup Boursin cheese (or a cream cheese with
   garlic and herbs of your choice)
½ lb. smoked salmon, thinly sliced
½ small red onion, thinly sliced
¼ cup capers, rinsed
1 loaf ciabatta bread, sliced in half lengthwise
olive oil, for brushing

Heat the panini press. Spread the cheese
on both cut sides of the bread and arrange
the salmon and red onion on one side and
sprinkle with capers. Close and brush both
sides with olive oil.

Cook in the panini press for 3–4 minutes,
until the crust is golden and crispy. Cut into
bite-size squares or rectangles. Wrap with
paper and tie with twine. Serve warm.

Blue Cheese Terrine

SERVES 10
16 oz. firm blue cheese, crumbled
2½ oz. soft fresh goat cheese
2½ oz. cream cheese, at room temperature
½ stick butter, at room temperature
2 tablespoons brandy
Rosemary Cashew Nuts and/or Roasted Grapes
   (see below), to garnish
crackers and bread, to serve
an 8½ x 2½ inch cake pan, lightly oiled, lined
with plastic wrap to extend over
the edges

Combine the blue cheese, goat cheese,
cream cheese, and butter in a processor
and blend until smooth. Stir in the brandy.
Spoon the mixture into the prepared loaf pan
and refrigerate overnight.

Carefully unmold the cheese onto a serving
platter and top with Rosemary Cashew Nuts
and/or Roasted Grapes. Serve with crackers
and bread.

ROASTED GRAPES

SERVES 6–8
1 lb. red and/or green seedless grapes
2 tablespoons balsamic vinegar
1 tablespoon grapeseed oil

Preheat the oven to 375°F. Spread the grape
clusters out on a baking sheet. Drizzle with
vinegar and oil. Roast in the preheated oven
for 12 minutes or until the grape skins are
slightly blistered. Serve the grapes warm or
at room temperature.

ROSEMARY CASHEW NUTS

SERVES 6–8
½ cup finely chopped rosemary
2 tablespoons olive oil
1 lb. roasted and salted cashew nuts

Preheat the oven to 450°F. On a baking
sheet, toss the rosemary and oil with
the nuts. Roast in the preheated oven for
10–12 minutes. Serve the nuts warm or
at room temperature.

Chocolate & Coffee Party

MENU FOR 8–10 GUESTS

APERITIF	White Russian
DESSERT COFFEE BAR	Create Your Own Flavorful Gourmet Coffee
DESSERT TABLE	Torta Cavour

With Kahlúa Crème

Chocolate Brownie Tarts

Ginger Crème Sandwich Cookies

With Ginger Crème Filling

Miniature Pavlova

With Passion Fruit Crème

Chocolate Espresso Malts

Served in Chocolate Cups

Pure Indulgence

Chocolate and coffee—two of the most favored and craved food items in the world. Chocolate releases endorphins in the brain and makes you feel happy. Caffeine in coffee gives you energy. What great elements for a party! Not only are they great food elements, they make for beautiful décor. So for this party we are making it look as good as it tastes by doing everything in tones of chocolate, coffee, and cream.

Atop a brown suede-covered table, we let the chocolate do the talking as "eye candy" and accent our luscious desserts with a few small vases of hypericum, also known as coffee bean, brown roses, brown rudbekia, brown orchids, and chocolate cosmos (yes, they actually smell like chocolate!). We even use slabs of pure chocolate on the table for decoration. The dishware we have chosen has an appetizing chocolate-brown swirl pattern to complete the theme.

above An unexpected nosegay of thorny rudbekia matches the brown and gold tones of our chocolate-inspired theme.

Torta Cavour
MAKES 1 LARGE 3-LAYER MERINGUE

For the meringues:
12 large egg whites, at room temperature
½ teaspoon cream of tartar
a pinch of salt
1½ teaspoons pure vanilla extract
3 cups sugar
¾ cup chestnut flour or cornstarch

For the filling:
4 cups heavy cream
1 cup granulated sugar
¼ cup Kahlúa or Amaretto
1½ cups toasted slivered almonds
14 oz. semisweet chocolate, coarsely chopped
parchment paper with 3 x 10-inch
    traced circles
3 baking sheets
a pastry bag

Preheat the oven to 200°F or lowest setting.
Place the egg whites, cream of tartar, salt,
and vanilla in a large mixing bowl and beat
until frothy and the mixture holds soft peaks.
Gradually beat in sugar about ¼ cup at a
time. Continue beating at high speed until
the whites are glossy and thick. Pour the
chestnut flour over the egg whites and fold
in with a plastic spatula just until combined.

Fill a pastry bag with the meringue. Place
the tip of the bag on the perimeter of one
of the parchment circles and start piping the
meringue. Continue piping in decreasing
circles to the center. Fill all circles alike.
Place in the preheated oven for about
2 hours, until the meringues are crisp and
dry. Allow to cool before filling. To make the
filling, put the cream in a large, chilled bowl
and whip it, gradually beating in the sugar
until soft peaks form. Add the liqueur a little
at a time and beat until medium peaks form.

To assemble, place a meringue round on
a serving tray. Spread with some cream and
sprinkle with about ⅓ of the almonds and
chocolate and press lightly into the cream.
Repeat with another layer of meringue. Top
with the final layer and finish with remaining
cream, almonds, and chocolate. This dessert
may be prepared a day in advance and
allowed to mellow in the refrigerator.

Dessert Coffee Bar
Prepare decaffeinated and regular coffee
with dark espresso coffee beans. Select a
variety of liqueurs: Nocello, Kahlúa, Bailey's
Irish Cream, Amaretto, Godiva Chocolate
Liqueur, and various brandies. Choose
accompaniments such as coffee candies,
dark and white rock sugar swizzle sticks,
flavored sugar cubes, dark and white
chocolate chips, chocolate cigarettes,
cinnamon sticks, an array of rolled cookies,
whipped cream, and silver shakers filled with
cocoa, cinnamon, and confectioners' sugar.
Create an attractive display and let your
guests make their own artisanal coffee.

White Russian
MAKES 1 DRINK
1 fl oz. Kahlúa
1 fl oz. vodka
1 shot freshly-made espresso
½ cup lightly whipped cream
chocolate shavings, to garnish

Pour the Kahlúa, vodka, and espresso in a
serving glass of your choice and top with
whipped cream. Garnish with chocolate
shavings. Serve immediately.

Chocolate Brownie Tarts

SERVES 8-10

6 tablespoons unsalted butter
2 cups chopped semisweet chocolate
3 large eggs
1 cup granulated sugar
2 tablespoons instant coffee or 2 shots espresso
1 teaspoon pure vanilla extract
½ cup all-purpose flour
¼ teaspoon baking powder
¼ teaspoon salt
1 cup toasted pecans or hazelnuts, chopped
1 cup white or bittersweet chocolate chips
confectioners' sugar, to dust
fresh raspberries, to garnish
8-10 individual tart pans, greased
    and lightly floured

Preheat the oven to 350°F. Melt the butter and semisweet chocolate in a double boiler. Let cool. Beat the eggs, sugar, coffee, and vanilla extract together until the mixture is light and fluffy. Mix in the butter and chocolate mixture. Sift together the flour, baking powder, and salt. Fold the flour mixture into the egg and chocolate mixture. Add the nuts and chocolate chips. Spoon into the prepared tart pans. Bake in the preheated oven for 20–25 minutes. Serve warm, dusted with confectioners' sugar and garnished with fresh raspberries. Alternatively, add a scoop of vanilla ice cream and Hot Fudge Sauce (see page 74).

Ginger Crème Sandwich Cookies

MAKES 48 COOKIES

¾ cup unsalted butter
1 cup granulated sugar
¼ cup dark molasses
1 large egg
2 cups all-purpose flour
2 teaspoons baking soda
½ teaspoon salt
1 teaspoon confectioners' sugar
½ teaspoon ground cloves
1 teaspoon cinnamon

For the ginger crème:
2¼ cups confectioners' sugar
¼ cup crystallized ginger, finely chopped
¼ cup butter, at room temperature
a little cream or milk, to blend

Over medium heat, melt the butter in a large saucepan. Stir in the sugar and molasses. Add the egg and whisk well. Sift together the remaining ingredients and gradually stir into the molasses mixture until combined. Let chill for several hours in the refrigerator.

Preheat the oven to 375°F. Pinch and form the chilled dough into 1-inch balls. Place on a baking sheet and bake for 8–10 minutes.

To make the ginger crème, blend together the sugar, ginger, and butter. Add sufficient cream or milk to the mixture to obtain a spreadable consistency.

To assemble, spread a tablespoon of ginger crème on a cookie and top with another to make a sandwich. The filled cookies will stay crisp for several hours.

Miniature Pavlova with Passion Fruit Crème

MAKES 16-20 SMALL MERINGUES

8 large egg whites
¾ teaspoon salt
a pinch of cream of tartar
2 cups granulated sugar
1½ cups heavy cream
¾ cup confectioners' sugar
¾ cup prepared passion fruit purée
raspberries, figs, red currants, and cape
    gooseberries, to garnish
a few sprigs of mint, to garnish
a pastry bag
a baking sheet lined with parchment paper

Preheat oven to 200°F. Beat the egg whites, salt, and cream of tartar until soft peaks form. Gradually add the sugar until the mixture is glossy and holds stiff peaks. Spoon the meringue into a pastry bag and pipe 3-inch circles on the prepared baking sheet. Make a small indentation in each one with a spoon. Bake in the preheated oven for about 2 hours, until dry.

Whip the cream to medium peaks and gradually add the confectioners' sugar. Fold in the passion fruit purée. Fill the meringue shells with a few tablespoons of the cream and passion fruit mixture. Top with fruit and garnish with sprigs of mint.

Chocolate Espresso Malts

MAKES 8-10

1 pint bittersweet chocolate ice cream
2 tablespoons powdered malt
¼ cup milk
2 shots espresso, chilled
1 shot Kahlúa (optional)
8-10 espresso cups or edible chocolate cups*
whipped cream, chocolate shavings, and cinnamon
    sticks, to garnish

Put the ice cream, malt, milk, espresso, and Kahlúa in a blender and blend to combine. Pour into cups and garnish with whipped cream, chocolate shavings, and a cinnamon stick as a stirrer.

*Note: Edible chocolate espresso cups may be ordered from Chocolates à la Carte at www.chocolatesalacarte.com

right A topiary stork welcomes guests to the buffet table with moss and flowers nestled among the platters of food.

Baby Blues

Baby showers were primarily an American tradition until recent years but their popularity has spread around the world. We call this our "April Showers" party and use colorful inverted umbrellas, trimmed with flowers and raining streams of hyacinth blossoms. Of course pink and blue are the traditional colors but we push it a bit, departing from the customary pastels and moving into deeper shades of these hues. We even have pink and blue food and drinks! You could use this same umbrella theme for any spring party and your guests would be equally delighted. Upside-down umbrellas mounted to poles stand in the center of each table and a chain of separated hyacinth blossoms "drip" on to the table. The umbrellas have been covered in custom fabrics coordinated to the floral colors and at the base of each, is a bountiful garden of blooms. Nearly every available spring flower has been included, from roses and peonies to hydrangea and sweet peas. Inside each cone-shaped napkin roll is tucked a nosegay of sweet peas and at each place setting a charming individual teapot holds each guest's choice of tea and becomes their parting gift. An ivy topiary stork is perched on a nearby table as a symbol of the event.

Blue "Hpnotiq" Martini

MAKES 1 DRINK

6 fl oz. Hpnotiq
a splash of 7-up (or other clear lemonade)
freshly squeezed lemon juice, to taste

Add all the ingredients to a cocktail shaker filled with ice, shake, and strain into a cocktail glass rimmed with blue crystallized sugar.

Samantha Ruby's Sparkling Berry Lemonade

MAKES 1 COCKTAIL

6–8 fresh raspberries
2–3 fresh strawberries
granulated sugar, to taste
1½ fl oz. freshly squeezed lemon juice
2 fl oz. Simple Syrup (see page 73)
a dash of sparkling water

Muddle the fruit and sugar in a glass until juicy and the sugar has dissolved. Add the lemon juice and syrup, mix well. Add ice to the glass and top with sparkling water.

Creamy Goat Cheese with Roasted Tomatoes on a Crispy Spoon-shaped Cracker

MAKES 20 APPETIZERS

½ cup each of goat cheese and cream cheese
1 cup sun-dried tomatoes, finely chopped
basil leaves, finely chopped, to garnish

For the crispy spoon-shaped crackers:
½ lb. butter
1 cup all-purpose flour
½ teaspoon salt
¾ cup egg whites, about 4–5 whites
a sheet of lightweight plastic or cardboard
a sharp craft knife or scalpel
a baking sheet, lightly buttered

To make a spoon stencil, trace the shape of a teaspoon on a sheet of plastic. Carefully cut out the shape using a craft knife.

Preheat the oven to 350°F. Put the butter and salt in a mixer and blend. Gradually add the flour then slowly beat in the egg whites. Continue to mix until the dough is smooth. Place the stencil on a buttered baking sheet. Use a butter knife to spread one or two tablespoons of the batter into the stencil shape. Lift off the stencil and repeat this process to create 10 spoon shapes. Bake in the preheated oven for 10 minutes or until a light golden brown on the edges. Repeat this process to make another 10 crackers.

Put the goat and cream cheeses in a mixer and blend until well combined. To assemble, top each cracker with a little goat cheese mixture and tomatoes. Garnish with basil.

Mushroom Consommé

SERVES 10

1 oz. dried porcini mushrooms
6 cups chicken stock, warmed
1 lb. mushrooms, stems minced, caps sliced
3 tablespoons minced shallots
1 teaspoon salt
¼ teaspoon freshly ground black pepper
2 tablespoons dry sherry
1 tablespoon soy sauce
3 egg whites
2 egg shells, crumbled
freshly squeezed lemon juice, to taste
raw enoki mushrooms, to garnish

Soak the dried mushrooms in the pot of warmed chicken stock until soft. Discard any hard stems and strain the stock through cheesecloth to remove any sand. Pour the stock into a deep pot, add the soaked dried mushrooms, the chopped fresh mushroom stems, shallots, salt, and pepper. Bring just to a boil over medium heat. Reduce the heat and simmer for 40 minutes, skimming occasionally and keeping the level of liquid constant by adding more water. Remove from the heat and stir in the sherry and soy sauce.

Beat the egg whites with the egg shells in a large bowl. Whisking constantly, gradually add the broth to the whites. Return to the pot, place over medium heat, and whisk gently until the liquid is simmering. Let simmer for 15 minutes. The egg whites will coagulate and float to the top, forming a cap. Line a strainer or sieve with 2 layers of cheesecloth and set over large bowl. Gently ladle the consommé into the strainer, pressing the liquid through with the back of the ladle. Season to taste.

Combine 2 cups water and the lemon juice in a small saucepan and bring to a boil. Add the sliced mushroom caps and simmer for 2 minutes. Drain well. Transfer to a clean stockpot and add the strained consommé. Bring to a simmer. Ladle into bowls and garnish with uncooked enoki mushrooms.

Chicken and Pesto Salad with Arugula

SERVES 8–10

8 chicken breasts or thighs, cooked and shredded
1½ cups Pesto Vinaigrette (see page 147)
2 bunches watercress, stems removed
1 lb. baby arugula
½ cup toasted pine nuts
¾ cup Parmesan cheese, grated
½ cup sun-dried tomatoes
sea salt and freshly ground pepper

In a large salad bowl, combine the chicken, pesto vinaigrette, watercress, and arugula and lightly toss. Taste and add salt and pepper, if needed. Garnish with the pine nuts, Parmesan cheese, and sun-dried tomatoes and serve immediately.

Note: A favorite salad with our clients—the salad will wilt quickly so be sure to combine the ingredients just as you serve the salad.

BASIC PESTO
MAKES 1 CUP
2 cups basil leaves
2 garlic cloves, crushed
¼ cup pine nuts, toasted
½ cup extra virgin olive oil
½ cup grated Parmesan cheese
sea salt to taste

Combine the basil, salt, garlic, and pine nuts in a food processor or blender. While the machine is running, slowly add the oil. Keep in a covered container with some extra oil on top in the refrigerator. When ready to use, add the Parmesan cheese.

PESTO VINAIGRETTE
1 cup Pesto (see recipe above)
¼ cup white wine vinegar
freshly squeezed juice of 1 lemon
⅓ cup extra virgin olive oil
sea salt and freshly ground black pepper

In a bowl, whisk together the pesto, vinegar, lemon juice, and olive oil. Season to taste with salt and pepper. The Pesto Vinaigrette is a little heavier than a usual one so use sparingly and add just before serving.

Chocolate Cupcakes
MAKES 12 CUPCAKES
3 oz. bittersweet chocolate, chopped
1¾ cups all-purpose or cake flour
1½ cups sugar
1 teaspoon baking soda
1 teaspoon salt
1 cup sour cream or crème fraîche
6 tablespoons unsalted butter, at room temperature
2 large eggs
1½ teaspoons pure vanilla extract
¼ cup hot coffee
Vanilla Buttercream Frosting (see right)
a 12-cup cupcake pan, liberally buttered
   and fitted with paper liners

Preheat the oven to 350°F. In a double boiler melt the chocolate. Remove from the heat and stir until smooth. In a separate large bowl, sift the flour, sugar, baking soda, and salt. Add the sour cream and butter and

beat for 2 minutes. Add the melted chocolate, eggs, vanilla, and coffee. Beat until combined. Scrape down the bowl. Pour batter into the cupcake pans about two-thirds full. Bake in the preheated oven for 15–20 minutes or until the center of a cake springs back when lightly pressed. Let cool in the pan for 10 minutes. Turn out and allow to cool completely before frosting.

Vanilla Cupcakes
MAKES 12 CUPCAKES
1½ sticks unsalted butter, room temperature
1½ cups sugar
2 cups all-purpose or cake flour
2 teaspoons baking powder
¼ teaspoon salt
6 large egg whites
¾ cup milk
1 tablespoon pure vanilla extract
Vanilla Buttercream Frosting (see below)
a 12-cup cupcake pan, liberally buttered
   and fitted with paper liners

Preheat the oven to 350°F. In a large mixing bowl, beat the butter and sugar together until light and fluffy. In a separate bowl, sift together the flour, baking powder, and salt. Combine the egg whites, milk, and vanilla. Alternating the flour mixture and egg mixture, beginning and ending with the flour mixture, mix both into the butter and sugar mixture, scraping down the bowl frequently.

Spoon the mixture into cupcake pan and bake for 15–20 minutes, until the center of a cake springs back when lightly pressed. Let cool in the pan for 10 minutes. Turn out and allow to cool completely before frosting.

VANILLA BUTTERCREAM FROSTING
1½ lbs. unsalted butter, at room temperature
3 cups confectioners' sugar
2 tablespoons pure vanilla extract
a pinch of salt
a few drops each of red and blue food coloring

Put the butter in a bowl and slowly beat while gradually adding sugar. Scrape down the sides of the bowl and add the vanilla extract and salt. Continue to beat until the mixture is fluffy. Transfer half the frosting to a second bowl. Add sufficient blue food

coloring to one and red to the other, to create the desired shade. Beat well. When the cupcakes are completely cooled, frost with the Vanilla Buttercream.

Note: Colored "dots" may be achieved by spooning a small amount of buttercream in a pastry bag fitted with a small round tip. Pipe little dots on each cupcake.

Checkerboard Cookies for a Baby Boy or Girl
MAKES 20 COOKIES
½ cup unsalted butter or shortening
1 cup granulated sugar
1½ teaspoons pure vanilla extract
2½ cups all-purpose flour
2 egg (yolk only of 1)
a few drops of blue or red food coloring
¼ cup cocoa powder mixed with 1 tablespoon milk
   or water (needed for boy cookies only)
2 baking sheets, lightly greased or lined
   with parchment paper
1¾-inch square cookie cutter

Preheat the oven to 350°F. Place the butter, sugar, and vanilla in a mixer or food processor and blend until smooth. Add the flour, egg, and egg yolk and continue mixing until a dough just forms.

Remove half the dough. For a girl baby shower, add red food coloring to reach desired shade, leaving the second half of the dough plain. For a boy baby shower, add blue food coloring to half to reach desired shade, and with the second half, add the cocoa and milk and blend to combine.

Roll the doughs out between two sheets of parchment paper to ¼ inch thickness. Cut into squares with a square cookie cutter. Arrange two squares of each color in a checkerboard pattern (as shown opposite) on a prepared baking sheet. Bake in the preheated oven for 10–12 minutes. Remove from the oven, transfer to a wire rack, and let cool completely before serving. These cookies are best eaten on the day they are baked but will keep for 2–3 days if stored in an air-tight container.

A Pink Luncheon

MENU FOR 6–8 GUESTS

APERITIF   Pink Hibiscus Lemonade

BUFFET   The Great Big "Create Your Own" Salad Bar

Baby Arugula with Watercress, Mixed Baby Greens, and Fresh Pea Shoots,

Marinated and Roasted Red, Yellow, and Green Tomatoes

A Variety of Fresh Cherry Tomatoes and Avocado Slices

Jicama, Marinated Artichokes, and Artichoke Crisps

Julienned Red and Yellow Bell Peppers

Mushrooms, Edamame, and Fresh Peas

Fresh Blood Orange, Pink Grapefruit, and Orange Segments

Fresh Corn Kernels in a Lime Marinade

St. Agur Blue Cheese, Mt. Tam Chevre, and String Cheese

Marinated Olives with Fresh Herbs

"The Kitchen's" cheesy croutons

A Selection of Salad Dressings including Gorgonzola, Balsamic,

Pomegranate Molasses Vinaigrette, and Meyer Lemon Vinaigrette

Grilled Chicken Strips
In a Chimichuri Sauce

Italian Seafood Salad
With a Meyer Lemon Vinaigrette

Edamame Rice Salad
With a Wasabi Vinaigrette

DESSERT   Berry Upside-Down Cake

Oeufs à la Neige

Almond Cake
With Pink Mascarpone Cream

Pretty in Pink

Decidedly feminine, pink is a perfect choice for a ladies' luncheon in this stunning rose garden at the height of its bloom. By combining mixed shades of pink, from pale to hot in both the flowers and the food, we create a lively ambience that sets the stage for a fun, rambunctious party. Sitting at pink tables, starting with pink hibiscus lemonade, and ending with a variety of pink desserts, the guests at this party will bask in a blush glow from start to finish. After all, everyone looks good in pink!

Setting this party in a rose garden inevitably establishes roses as the secondary theme. Not much can compete with a perfect rose unless it's dozens upon dozens of them, so that is what we are using. We include every variety of pink rose we could find, from plump Yves Piaget garden roses to miniature spray roses, filling the table in an abundant display with dashes of lime green viburnum and wild raspberry sprigs as fresh accents. A rose pattern adorns the antique Limoges china and a small pink rose is attached to each place card. If, as they say, pink makes one feel younger and happy, then your guests will almost certainly never want to leave.

To make the Hibiscus Concentrate, put all the ingredients in a saucepan and bring to a boil. Reduce the heat and simmer for a few minutes. Let cool and strain. The concentrate may be kept in the refrigerator for several days. To make the hibiscus lemonade, pour all of the ingredients into a pitcher. Fill the glasses with ice and pour over. Garnish with lavender sprigs and citrus wheels.

Italian Seafood Salad
SERVES 8-10
2 lbs. raw scallops, white parts only
2 lbs. raw shrimp
1 lb. raw calamari, sliced
24 green-lipped mussels
2 lobster tails
2 cups sliced celery rib
1 cup sliced red and yellow cherry tomatoes
1 avocado, chopped into ½-inch pieces
½ cup Meyer Lemon Vinaigrette (see opposite)
1 cup micro sprouts, to garnish

For the stock:
2 unwaxed lemons, sliced
2 bay leaves
1 onion, chopped
1 cup white wine
1 tablespoon peppercorns
1 teaspoon salt
3 quarts water

Meyer Lemon Vinaigrette:
⅓ cup Meyer or Eureka lemon juice
3 teaspoons honey
1 cup virgin olive oil
2 teaspoons shallots, finely diced
½ teaspoon salt
½ teaspoon pepper

To make the Meyer Lemon Vinaigrette, put all of the ingredients a bowl and whisk to combine. Refrigerate until ready to use.

To make the stock, place all the ingredients in a large pot and bring to a boil. Add the seafood and simmer until opaque. Remove the seafood from the stock using a slotted spoon. Transfer to a bowl, cover, and set aside. Add the celery to the reserved stock and simmer for one minute. Add to the bowl of seafood and chill in the refrigerator for 1–2 hours. When ready to serve, add the

above Wild raspberries peeking out from under pink roses make this floral arrangement look good enough to eat.

Pink Hibiscus Lemonade
MAKES 4 QUARTS
2 cups Hibiscus Lavender Concentrate (see below)
1½–2 cups freshly squeezed lemon juice
2 cups sugar
2½ quarts water
6–8 fresh lavender sprigs, to garnish
citrus wheels, to garnish
8–10 serving glasses

Hibiscus Lavender Concentrate:
½ cup dried hibiscus (dried hibiscus flowers may be found in a herb catalogue or Chinese markets)
2 cups water
8 sprigs fresh lavender, to garnish (optional)

tomatoes and avocado and lightly combine with Meyer Lemon Vinaigrette. Garnish with micro sprouts.

Grilled Chicken Strips in a Chimichuri Sauce

SERVES 8-10

6 grilled chicken breasts, cut into strips

For the chimichuri sauce:
1 cup coarsely chopped cilantro
1 cup coarsely chopped parsley
¼ cup coarsely chopped mint
3 garlic cloves, minced
4 shallots, minced
¼ cup red wine vinegar
a pinch of dried hot red pepper flakes
a pinch of dried oregano
a pinch of ground cumin
¾ cup olive oil
sea salt and freshly ground black pepper

To make the chimichuri sauce, put all the ingredients in a food processor and blend until well combined. Season to taste with salt and pepper. Drizzle the chicken with the chimichuri sauce. Any left over will keep in an airtight container in the refrigerator for 2–3 days.

Edamame Rice Salad

SERVES 8-10

2 cups long-grain rice, steamed with salt to taste
2 cups cooked and shelled edamame beans
2 small cucumbers, peeled, seeded, and diced
½ cup finely diced celery from inner stalks
¼ cup thinly sliced scallions
coarse salt
chopped mint, to taste
1 cup micro sprouts, if desired
2 ripe medium avocados, peeled, pitted, and diced
salt and freshly ground black pepper

For the Wasabi Vinaigrette:
½ cup vegetable or sunflower oil
¼ cup rice vinegar
2 teaspoons sugar
wasabi powder or paste, to taste

To make the Wasabi Vinaigrette, put the oil, vinegar and sugar in a bowl and whisk to combine. Add wasabi to taste.

Add the Wasabi Vinaigrette to the cooked and cooled rice and stir in the remaining ingredients, adding the avocados last. Season to taste with salt and pepper and serve immediately

Berry Upside-Down Cake

SERVES 8-10

⅓ cup unsalted butter, plus 1 tablespoon melted and cooled
¾ cup brown sugar
2 pints blackberries, raspberries, or blueberries
1 teaspoon almond extract
4 eggs, separated
1 cup all-purpose flour
1 teaspoon baking powder
¼ teaspoon salt
1 cup granulated sugar
2 cups fresh berries, to serve
½ cup red currant jelly, melted (optional)
whipped cream, Dulce de Leche, or vanilla ice cream, to serve

a 9–10 inch round baking pan, 2½-inch sides

Preheat the oven to 350°F. Put the ⅓ cup butter in the baking pan. Place it in the oven to melt the butter. Remove from the oven and add the brown sugar. Stir and return to the oven for 5 minutes, stirring once or twice, then remove. Spread the berries in a single layer on the sugar.

Whisk the melted butter and almond extract into the egg yolks and set aside. In another bowl, sift together the flour, baking powder, and salt. Beat the egg whites on medium speed until they just form peaks. Do not overbeat. Fold the granulated sugar into the egg whites a fourth at a time. Then fold in egg yolk mixture a fourth at a time. Finally fold in flour mixture a fourth at a time. Pour the batter over the berries and spread evenly to form a smooth surface.

Bake for about 30 minutes. A toothpick inserted in the center of the cake should come out clean when it is ready. Let stand for at least 10 minutes before unmolding. Additional fresh berries may be added to the cake before serving. Glaze these with the melted red currant jelly. Serve with whipped cream, Dulce de Leche, or vanilla ice cream.

Oeufs à la Neige

SERVES 6-8

4 large egg whites, at room temperature
1 teaspoon pure vanilla extract
¼ teaspoon cream of tartar
¼ teaspoon salt
⅔ cup superfine sugar
1 pint fresh red berries of your choice

For the Raspberry Crème Anglaise:
6 egg yolks
⅔ cup sugar
1½ cups hot milk
1 tablespoon pure vanilla extract
3 tablespoons unsalted butter
¼ cup puréed raspberries
a 12 x 12 inch baking pan
6-8 10-oz Martini glasses or similar

Preheat the oven to 375°F. Beat the egg whites until foamy. Add the vanilla, cream of tartar, and salt, and beat until soft peaks form. Gradually beat in the sugar. Increase the speed to high and beat until thick and glossy peaks form. Transfer the mixture to a baking pan. Bake in the preheated oven for 10–15 minutes, until golden brown.

Meanwhile, make the Raspberry Crème Anglaise. Over a double boiler, whisk the egg yolks adding the sugar gradually, until the mixture is fluffy and pale yellow. Whisk in the milk and vanilla. Remove from the heat and whisk in the butter. Let cool and fold in the raspberry purée.

Spoon some Raspberry Crème Anglaise into each serving dish. Top with a large scoop of meringue and garnish with fresh berries.

Almond Cake with Pink Mascarpone Cream

MAKES 1 LARGE CAKE

8 oz. ready-made almond paste
½ cup unsalted butter, softened
¼ cup sugar
3 eggs
2 teaspoons finely grated lemon zest
2 tablespoons Grand Marnier, or Amaretto
¼ cup all-purpose flour
½ teaspoon baking powder
balsamic-marinated strawberries and candied
   orange peel, to garnish (optional)
an 8-inch cake pan, lightly buttered
   and floured

For the Pink Mascarpone Cream:
1 lb. mascarpone cheese
3 tablespoons sugar
¼ cup Grand Marnier
¼ cup puréed raspberries
2 teaspoons orange zest
2 cups whipped cream

Preheat the oven to 350°F. To make the cake, put the almond paste, butter, and sugar in a bowl and mix. One at a time, beat in the eggs, followed by the lemon zest and Grand Marnier. Sift the flour and baking powder together, and add to the almond mixture until just combined. Pour the batter into the prepared cake pan and bake in the preheated oven for 35–40 minutes, until a toothpick inserted in the center of the cake comes out clean. Let cool on a rack before removing the cake from the pan.

To make the Mascarpone Cream, beat together the mascarpone, sugar, Grand Marnier, puréed raspberries, and orange zest until well combined and fluffy. Fold in the whipped cream. When ready to serve, spoon onto slices of the cake and garnish with strawberries and candied orange peel.

A Moroccan-style Party

MENU FOR 8–10

APERITIF	Orange Blossom Cocktail
TO BE PASSED	Moroccan Savory Stars
	With a Fresh Tomato Chutney
FAMILY STYLE	Baked Eggplants with Chermoula Sauce
	Fruity Chicken Tagine
	Beet and Cantaloupe Salad
	With a Citrus Vinaigrette
	Moroccan-style Carrots
	Roasted Herb-filled Leg of Lamb
	With a Fresh Mint Pistou
	Wedding Rice
DESSERT	Fromage Blanc with Figs
	With Honey and Toasted Almonds

"Mark's Garden designed gorgeous arrangements of orange roses that
I used throughout my film 'Hanging up' to perfectly accent the mood
of various scenes."

Diane Keaton

Casablanca Revisited

opposite page left A delicious feast is set out on an authentic-looking pavilion in Beverly Hills. *opposite page right* Towers of figs, dates, currants, and apricots stand majestically on the table.

Come with us to the casbah. Not everyone is lucky enough to be able to throw a Moroccan party on an authentic-looking pavilion such as this one we found on the former estate of set designer Tony Duquette. But we were and it became a fantastic inspiration. We wanted to create the same sense of mystery and romance that not only was depicted in legendary films of the past but actually still exists in nooks and crannies off the convoluted streets of Moroccan cities today. Our further aim was to capture a little of the magic of the place that has sparked artists like Delacroix and Matisse and create an artistic environment of our own.

In selecting our color palette, we were further influenced by the colorful food on our menu and the wide array of the traditional spices used in this cuisine. Dominating the main table are tall, vividly colored spires of pavéd fruit combined with traditional flowers. Included are dried dates, figs, apricots, peaches, and papaya alternated with yellow button mums and cymbidium orchids. A collage of spicy red, orange, and yellow tones are mixed with earthy browns and touches of vivid blue. With the family-style setup and the abundance of food, our setting spills over to side tables and even to the floor that we cover with multi-colored rose petals and votive candles. We have hung strands of orchid blossoms from the arches in the background and tucked marigolds among the heaping dishes of food. An antique brass coffee urn serves as a vase for exotic flowering vines. Traditional Moroccan tea glasses are used for drinking as well as votive candles which will burn late into the night if this party is anything like the ones that take place in Tangier. All in all it becomes an incredible banquet for the eyes and the soul as much as the stomach.

Orange Blossom Cocktail

MAKES 1 DRINK

1½ fl oz. orange-infused vodka
a splash of freshly squeezed lemon juice
a splash of freshly squeezed orange juice
1–2 drops orange blossom water
1½ fl oz. apricot nectar
2 fl oz. unfiltered apple juice
slice of orange, to garnish

Put all the ingredients in a shaker filled with ice and shake. Pour into a Moroccan tea glass or tumbler to serve.

Moroccan Savory Stars

MAKES 36-48 STARS

2 cups quick-cooking polenta
vegetable oil, for frying
8 oz. mild goat cheese, at room temperature
8 oz. cream cheese, at room temperature
2 cups Fresh Tomato Chutney (see below)
mint leaves, to garnish
a baking sheet with sides, greased
a star cookie cutter

Cook the polenta according to the package directions. Spread onto the prepared baking sheet and let cool. Cut into small stars. In a large, deep skillet, heat 1–2 inches of oil to 250°F. Fry the polenta stars until they are light golden brown and crisp. This may be done in advance and the stars reheated for a few minutes in a preheated 375°F oven.

Put the goat cheese and cream cheese in a bowl and blend. Top each warm star with 1 teaspoon cheese mixture and 1 teaspoon tomato chutney. Garnish with a mint leaf. Serve immediately.

FRESH TOMATO CHUTNEY

MAKES 2 QUARTS

4 oz. ginger root, peeled and chopped
1 cup cider vinegar
2 cups brown sugar
2 cups granulated sugar
2 lemons, sliced
1 tablespoon ground cinnamon
1 tablespoon ground cumin
½ teaspoon ground cloves
¼ teaspoon freshly ground black pepper
1 teaspoon sea salt
2 cups each yellow and red cherry tomatoes, halved
1 cup mint leaves, finely chopped

Put the first 10 ingredients in a pan with 1 cup water. Bring to a boil, reduce the heat, and simmer until slightly thickened, stirring occasionally. Remove from the heat and strain. Add the tomatoes and mint.

The chutney may be made ahead of time and refrigerated for up to 2 days. Any extra chutney is a good topping for grilled chicken breast or fish fillet.

Baked Eggplants with Chermoula Sauce

SERVES 8-10

6–8 Japanese eggplants, trimmed and cut lengthwise
3–4 red bell peppers, seeded and quartered
olive oil, for brushing
¼ cup chopped thyme
¾ cup Chermoula Sauce (see below)
½ cup roasted and salted Spanish Marcona almonds
mint leaves, torn
sea salt and freshly ground black pepper
a baking sheet, lined with parchment paper

Preheat the oven to 375°F. Put the eggplants and peppers on a lined baking sheet. Brush with olive oil, sprinkle with thyme, and season with salt and pepper. Bake in the preheated oven for 25–30 minutes, or until the eggplants are tender. Arrange on a warmed platter and drizzle with Chermoula Sauce. Scatter the almonds and mint leaves over the top to garnish. Serve warm or at room temperature.

CHERMOULA SAUCE

MAKES 1 CUP

1 white onion, chopped
6 garlic cloves, minced
2 teaspoons ground cumin
1 teaspoon paprika
½ teaspoon saffron threads, crushed and steeped in 2 tablespoons hot water
½ cup flatleaf parsley
½ cup cilantro
6 tablespoons olive oil
6 tablespoons freshly squeezed lemon juice
sea salt and freshly ground black pepper

Put all the ingredients in a food processor and blend to combine. Serve the sauce at room temperature. Any left over can be stored for 2–3 days in the refrigerator.

Fruity Chicken Tagine

SERVES 8–10

2 teaspoons ground cinnamon
2 teaspoons ground ginger
2 teaspoons turmeric
2 pinches of saffron threads
1 teaspoon sea salt
1 teaspoon freshly ground black pepper
½ cup butter or vegetable oil
8 chicken breasts, bone-in
4 chicken thighs, bone-in
3–4 onions, chopped
2–3 garlic cloves, peeled and crushed
2–4 cups chicken stock or water
1 lb. dried apricots, sliced
1 lb. dates or prunes, pitted and sliced
2 cups salted and roasted Spanish Marcona almonds
cinnamon sticks and cilantro sprigs, to garnish
a tagine (optional)

Combine the cinnamon, ginger, turmeric, saffron, salt, and pepper in a bowl. Rub the chicken pieces with the spice mixture.

Melt the butter in a large pot or tagine with lid. Sauté the chicken pieces until browned. Add the onions and garlic and sauté for another 5 minutes. Cover with chicken stock or water. Bring the mixture to a full boil, then reduce the heat for a low simmer. Cover and cook for about 30 minutes, until the chicken is tender. Remove the chicken from the pot, debone, and pull into medium-size pieces. Return to the pot and add the apricots and dates. Simmer for another 10 minutes. Add the almonds and serve garnished with cinnamon sticks and cilantro sprigs.

Beet and Cantaloupe Salad

SERVES 8–10

5 yellow beets, roasted and peeled
1 cantaloupe, peeled and seeded
5-oz. package Bull's Blood beet micro sprouts
¼ cup Citrus Vinaigrette (see right)
4 oz. soft chèvre or Mt. Tam cheese
sea salt and freshly ground black pepper

Slice or julienne the beets and cantaloupe, as similar in size as possible. On a platter, alternate beets and cantaloupe. Arrange the micro sprouts along the center, drizzle with Citrus Vinaigrette, and season with salt and pepper. Crumble or scatter the cheese over the top and serve at room temperature.

CITRUS VINAIGRETTE

the zest and freshly squeezed juice of 1 lemon, 1 lime, and 1 orange
¾ cup olive oil
sea salt and freshly ground black pepper

Whisk together the zest and juice of all the fruits. Slowly whisk in the olive oil. Season to taste with salt and pepper, and sharpen with more juice, if needed.

Moroccan-style Carrots

SERVES 8–10

8–10 young or baby carrots, tipped and peeled
1½ teaspoons ground cumin
1 teaspoon ground cinnamon
1 teaspoon ground ginger
2 teaspoons grated ginger root
dash of Tabasco or dried hot red pepper flakes
3 tablespoons freshly squeezed lemon or lime juice
½ cup olive oil
½ cup mint, finely chopped
sea salt and freshly ground black pepper

Steam or boil the carrots in salted water until tender. Drain and dust with cumin, cinnamon, ginger, ginger root, Tabasco, and lemon juice. Stir to coat well and marinate for at least an hour. Heat the oil in a large skillet over medium-high heat. Add the carrots, heat through, and season to taste with salt and pepper. Garnish with mint and serve immediately.

Roasted Herb-Filled Leg of Lamb

SERVES 8–10

a 5–6 lb. leg of lamb, boned and butterflied
3 tablespoons olive oil
2 garlic cloves, peeled and crushed
¼ cup chopped rosemary
¼ cup chopped thyme
Fresh Mint Pistou, to serve (see page 25)
sea salt and freshly ground black pepper
butcher's twine

Preheat the oven to 450°F. Trim the lamb of excess fat. Pound out as evenly as possible. Brush the lamb with olive oil and spread over the garlic, rosemary, and thyme. Season with salt and pepper. Roll up the lamb lengthwise and tie securely at 2-inch intervals with butcher's twine.

Put the lamb in a shallow roasting pan. For medium rare, roast until a thermometer inserted in the meat shows 125°F, about 45 minutes. Let rest for 10 minutes. Slice and serve with Fresh Mint Pistou.

Wedding Rice

SERVES 8–10

3 cups long grain rice
4½ cups chicken stock or water
1½ teaspoons sea salt
½ teaspoon saffron threads

Fruit and nut topping
¼ cup butter
½ cup Spanish Marcona almonds or pine nuts
¼ lb. dried apricots, sliced
¼ lb. dates, pitted and sliced
½ cup dried cranberries
½ cup golden raisins
¼ cup currants
1 cup pomegranate seeds (optional)

Put the rice, stock, salt, and saffron in a medium pan and bring to a boil. Reduce the heat, cover, and cook for 15 minutes until the liquid is absorbed and the rice tender.

To make the topping, melt the butter in a large frying pan. Add the almonds and sauté until lightly browned. Add the remaining ingredients and sauté until heated through. Stir often as this mixture burns easily.

When ready to serve, turn the rice out onto a large heated platter and cover with topping.

Fromage Blanc with Figs

SERVES 8–10

1 pint fromage blanc
½ pint crème fraîche or sour cream
2 egg whites
½ cup granulated sugar
1 teaspoon almond extract or Amaretto
honey, to drizzle
fresh figs and toasted slivered almonds, to serve

In a mixing bowl, combine the fromage blanc and crème fraîche. Beat the egg whites until soft peaks form, gradually adding the sugar. Fold the egg whites into the cheese mixture, then add the almond extract. Drizzle with honey and serve with figs and almonds.

50's Retro Party

MENU FOR 8-10 GUESTS

APERITIF Brent's Manhattan

BUFFET Grilled Vegetables

With Herb Marinade and Roasted Panko Bread Crumbs

Individual Meat Loaves

Rigatoni and Gruyère "Mac and Cheese"

With White Truffle Oil

Build-Your-Own Cobb Salad Bar

With Blue Cheese Dressing and Creamy Parmesan Dressing

Baked Potato Bar

With a Selection of Savory Toppings

DESSERT Cupcake and Candy Bar

Chocolate Cupcakes with Chocolate Sour Cream Icing

Orange Butter Cupcakes with Cream Cheese Coconut Frosting

Red Velvet Cupcakes

A Selection of Popular Retro Candies

Rock and Roll

Food from the 1950's has become the classic American food and its appeal is widespread. There is something about the simplicity of the 1950's itself that still evokes a happy feeling. Along with our inviting array of mouthwatering foods, we wanted to create an ambience that also evoked those happy days. This demands bright joyful flowers and nothing surpasses gerberas in this department.

Zany and madcap are good terms for the pavéd gerbera daisy heads covering the counters of this 50's-inspired kitchen. We like the "technicolor" image this table presents with the gradation of hot-toned flower heads weaving around and about the overflowing platters. The tall floral display of gerberas lined with stripes of pavéd button mums strikes just the right impudent pose for this casual tongue-in-cheek presentation.

above Bands of button mums surround the edges of the glass containers filled with popular candies of the period, like gumballs, jellybeans, malted balls, and licorice.

Caribbean Mood Dinner

MENU FOR 8-10 GUESTS

APERITIF	Mojito
TO BE PASSED	Jerk Chicken On a Plantain Tostone with a Mango Salsa
BUFFET	Beef Satays With a Black Bean Sauce
	"Moros y Cristianos" Black Beans, Tomatoes, and Steamed White Rice
	Garden Green Salad With a Passion Fruit Vinaigrette and Lotus Crisps
	Island Sweet Bread
DESSERT STATION	Fresh Pineapple Flambé Served over Vanilla Ice Cream, in a Lace Cookie Cup with Sesame Seeds
	Passion Fruit Crème Brûlée

Calypso Kick

The Caribbean is one of the great vacation playgrounds. Delicious food and sandy beaches are such a big part of the enjoyment of the inhabitants of those tropical isles that we were inspired to incorporate those elements into our décor. The hot spicy colors we've adopted, including reds, oranges, and yellows mixed with sexy pinks and purples, reflect their tasty cuisine and their zest for life against a backdrop of lush tropical greenery. This décor definitely says "Let's have a party!"

Succulent tropical fruit is incorporated with brilliant exotic flowers in the center of this table to create an unusual architectural centerpiece. Bright orange bird of paradise blooms are packed into crystal bowls lined with tropical leaves and surrounded with purple orchids and hot pink cockscomb. The fruit is stacked alternately between the floral pieces and some of the melons are sliced open to display splashes of the vivid colors of their interior. Orange clam shells and Kukui beads are added so the entire centerpiece spills across the table in a loose casual manner, with taper candles in gold candleholders and a miniature pineapple on its stem placed on each napkin to complete the eclectic playfulness of the Caribbean style.

Mojito

MAKES 1 DRINK

1 lime, sliced into wedges
2 heaping teaspoons brown sugar
1 small handful mint leaves
1 fl oz. white rum
a splash of soda water, to taste
½ fl oz. Meyer's Rum (dark)
mint sprig, to garnish
a muddler

Put all but 1 of the lime wedges and all the brown sugar and mint into a rocks glass and muddle well. Fill the glass with ice and add the white rum and soda water to taste. Pour in the Meyer's rum over the back of a spoon. Finish with a lime wedge and a sprig of mint.

Beef Satays

SERVES 8–10

1 cup soy sauce
1 cup pineapple juice
½ yellow onion, finely chopped
¼ cup sugar
¼ cup sambal or other hot chili sauce
1 jalapeño, seeds and vein removed, finely chopped
1 teaspoon ground nutmeg
1 tablespoon ground cinnamon
18–24 oz. beef steak, cut into thin strips
36–48 pearl onions
black bean sauce, to serve (see below)
sea salt and freshly ground black pepper
18–24 wood or metal skewers

Combine the first 8 ingredients and season to taste with salt and pepper. Skewer the beef strips and onions and marinate them in the mixture for at least 2 hours or overnight. Grill over a medium flame and serve immediately with Black Bean Sauce.

Note: At The Kitchen we use skirt steak or flap beef. Any tender steak will work well.

BLACK BEAN SAUCE

MAKES 4–5 CUPS

3 tablespoons vegetable oil
2 garlic cloves, minced
2 tablespoons minced ginger root
½ red onion, medium diced
2 cups canned black beans
¼ cup fermented black beans, soaked, rinsed, and coarsely chopped
1 each red, yellow, and green bell pepper, seeded and medium diced
2 tablespoons white wine
1 jalapeño, seeded and minced
2 cups cubed pineapple
½ cup peeled, pitted, and cubed mango
2 tablespoons light brown sugar
2–3 teaspoons curry powder
2 tablespoons freshly squeezed lime juice
3 scallions, sliced
¼ cup cilantro, chopped
sea salt
chicken stock, for thinning (optional)

Heat the oil in a large skillet over medium heat. Add the garlic and ginger until fragrant, about 30 seconds. Add the onion and sauté for 1 minute. Add the remaining ingredients except the lime juice, scallions, and cilantro. Bring to a simmer, but do not overcook as the peppers will lose their color. Remove from the heat and stir in the lime juice, scallions, and cilantro. Add salt to taste and a little chicken stock if the sauce is too thick.

Jerk Chicken

MAKES 15–20 APPETIZERS

1 tablespoon whole allspice
1 tablespoon black peppercorns
1 small cinnamon stick
2 cloves
1 teaspoon ground nutmeg
2 medium onions, coarsely chopped
4 scallions, chopped
½ Scotch bonnet or habanero pepper, seeded and chopped
4 cloves garlic, coarsely chopped
1 inch ginger root, peeled and sliced
½ cup tamarind paste
½ cup brown sugar
freshly squeezed juice of 2 limes
¼ cup extra virgin olive oil
3 chicken breasts, washed and dried
¼ cup Chipotle Sauce, plus extra if needed (see recipe on page 105)
cilantro sprigs, to garnish
mango salsa, to serve (see right)

a large bowl. Add the chipotle sauce and stir. Season and set aside.

To make the tostones, heat some oil to 350°F in a deep heavy skillet or wok. Peel the plantains and slice thinly using a mandoline. Fry the slices to a light golden brown and drain on paper towels. Sprinkle with sea salt flakes.

To assemble, put a large tablespoon of jerk chicken on the end of each tostone. Top with Mango Salsa and garnish with cilantro.

MANGO SALSA
2 ripe mangos, peeled, stoned, and finely diced
1 red bell pepper, seeded and finely diced
½ cup red onion, finely chopped
1 tablespoon jalapeno, finely diced
1½ teaspoons minced garlic
¾ cup rice wine vinegar
¼ cup finely chopped cilantro
sea salt and freshly ground black pepper

Put all the ingredients in a bowl and stir to combine. Season to taste with salt and pepper. Chill until ready to serve.

Moros y Cristianos
SERVES 8-10
2 tablespoons extra virgin olive oil
1 medium onion, finely chopped
1 tablespoon minced garlic
3 cups cooked or canned black beans, drained
1 cup chopped tomatoes
1 cup chicken or vegetable stock
3-4 cups Steamed White Rice (see below)
sea salt and freshly ground black pepper

Put the oil in a large, deep skillet over medium heat. Add the onion, season, and cook until soft, about 4–5 minutes. Stir in the garlic, beans, tomatoes, and stock. Turn the heat to medium/high and cook, stirring, for about 7–8 minutes, or until the beans are hot and most of the liquid is evaporated. To serve, put the hot white rice on a platter and top with the black bean mixture.

STEAMED WHITE RICE
5 cups water, chicken stock, or vegetable stock
2 cups long-grain rice
2 teaspoons sea salt

Put the water, rice, and salt in a large pan and bring to a boil. Cover and reduce the heat. Simmer until all the liquid is absorbed and the rice is tender, about 20 minutes.

Garden Green Salad with Passion Fruit Vinaigrette
SERVES 8-10
8 cups or handfuls mixed baby greens
2 mangos, peeled, pitted, and cut into bite-size cubes
1 pineapple, peeled, cored, and cut into bite-size cubes
2 papayas, peeled, seeded, and cut into bite-size cubes
6 kiwis, peeled and sliced
2 avocados, peeled, pitted, and sliced
sea salt and freshly ground black pepper

PASSION FRUIT VINAIGRETTE
¼ cup prepared passion fruit purée
¼ cup freshly squeezed lemon juice
¾ cup extra virgin olive oil
sea salt and freshly ground black pepper

LOTUS CRISPS
corn or vegetable oil, for frying
2 lotus fruits

To make the vinaigrette, put the passion fruit purée and lemon juice in a bowl and beat to combine. While beating, slowly add in the olive oil. Season to taste with salt and pepper.

To make the lotus crisps, heat the oil to 350°F in a heavy, deep skillet. Thinly slice the lotus on a mandoline. Fry in oil until light golden brown and drain on paper towels.

To assemble the salad, put the greens in a large bowl. Season with salt and pepper and toss with some of the Passion Fruit Vinaigrette. Mound the greens on a serving

PLANTAIN TOSTONE
corn or vegetable oil, for frying
2-3 plantains, green or yellow, not dark and ripe
sea salt flakes

In a sauté pan over medium heat, add the allspice, peppercorns, cinnamon stick, cloves, and nutmeg. Toast for 1–2 minutes, but do not allow them to burn. Put in a clean coffee or spice grinder and process to a powder. Put the remaining ingredients, except for the chicken and chipotle sauce, in a food processor or blender, add the spice mix, and purée until smooth. Add more oil if needed and season with salt and pepper.

Put the chicken breasts in a ziplock bag, add the jerk spice mixture, and marinate in the refrigerator for at least 2 hours or overnight if possible. Preheat the oven to 350°F. Put the chicken in a baking dish or roasting pan and bake in the preheated oven for 20–25 minutes or until cooked through. Once the chicken is cool, shred the meat, and put it in platter. Surround with the fruit. Drizzle more Passion Fruit Vinaigrette over the fruit and top with sliced avocado and lotus crisps.

Island Sweet Bread

MAKES 1 LOAF

2 tablespoons dry yeast
¼ cup instant potato flakes
⅔ cup boiling water
⅔ cup sugar
½ cups butter
¼ cup powdered milk
3 eggs
1 teaspoon salt
½ teaspoon pure vanilla extract
¼ teaspoon lemon extract
5 cups all-purpose flour

Preheat the oven to 350°F. Dissolve the yeast in ⅓ cup warm water in a large mixer. Mix the potato flakes, ⅔ cup boiling water, sugar, butter, and powdered milk in a separate bowl. Set aside to let cool. When lukewarm, add this to the yeast mixture and stir to combine.

Add the eggs one at a time, then the salt, vanilla, and lemon extract. Add the flour and mix well. Transfer to a large bowl and leave in a warm place until doubled in size, about 1 hour. When risen, form into your desired loaf shape and bake in the preheated oven for 45–55 minutes, until risen and golden brown.

Fresh Pineapple Flambé

SERVES 8-10

½ cup butter
½ cup brown sugar
½ pineapple, peeled, cored, and cut into
    medium chunks
¾–1 cup dark rum
8–10 Lace Cookie Cups (see right)
vanilla ice cream, to serve
edible flowers, to garnish (optional)

In a large skillet, cook the butter and sugar over medium heat, stirring until the sugar is

dissolved. Add the pineapple and reduce the heat to low. Cook until the pineapple is browned on one side. Turn and cook until browned and soft. Carefully add the rum and set it alight.

Scoop vanilla ice cream into the lace cookie cups and spoon the cooked pineapple over the top. Drizzle with the rum liquid from the skillet, garnish with a chunk of pineapple and a flower, if using, and serve immediately.

LACE COOKIE CUPS

1 quantity Lace Cookies (see page 41) with
2 tablespoons sesame seeds
a 12-cup muffin pan or 10 individual cup molds,
    lightly oiled or buttered

Follow the method for making Lace Cookies on page 41 but sprinkle the cookies with sesame seeds before putting them in the oven. When the cookies are baked, but still warm, place each one into the prepared pan and use your fingers to press into the mold to form a cup shape. When cool, gently tip the cookie cups out. Use the cups as an edible serving dish for Fresh Pineapple Flambé (see left) or any flavor ice cream with the sauce of your choice. The cookies will keep for up to 1 week stored in an airtight container.

Passion Fruit Crème Brûlée

SERVES 8-10

12 large egg yolks
⅔ cup granulated sugar
1 vanilla bean, halved lengthwise
4 cups heavy cream, chilled
a pinch of salt
½ cup prepared passion fruit purée
8–12 teaspoons turbinado sugar
slices of fresh fig and/or kiwi, to garnish (optional)
8–10 ramekins
a deep baking dish

Preheat the oven to 300°F. Mix the egg yolks and granulated sugar in a large bowl until combined. Slice the vanilla bean lengthwise and scrape out the seeds with the back of a

knife. Add the seeds and bean to the heavy cream. Heat the cream and vanilla to a scalding point, then gradually pour into the egg mixture while beating constantly. Add the salt and passion fruit purée. Pour the mixture through a strainer.

Divide the custard into ramekins and put in a deep baking dish. Fill the baking dish with hot water three-fourths of the way up the sides of the ramekins. Bake in the preheated oven or 25–35 minutes.

Remove from the oven and let cool to room temperature, then refrigerate until well chilled. When ready to serve, spread an even layer of turbinado sugar over the top of each custard. Caramelize with a blowtorch or place under a preheated broiler for 3–4 minutes, until the sugar has caramelized and formed a topping.

Garnish with slices of fresh fig or kiwi, if using, and serve at room temperature.

Floral Tips

USING COLOR

Let's face it. Not everybody has good color sense. For inexperienced floral designers one of the best rules is to design your arrangement with one color even if you mix types of flowers. With all white flowers you can easily succeed in making a beautiful arrangement. If you really feel adventurous, add a dash of green. If you are newly venturing into color, first try all pink or all red but feel free to vary the shades. If you want to use orange for instance, combine peach and apricot tones. Soon you will be expanding to mixing colors. When you do, it is best to stay with all pastels or all hot bright tones. Always think about your color combinations. People respond to color and it often has more impact than the type of flowers you use. With practice you will learn what combinations work. Talented floral designers are artists who "paint" with color.

TROPICAL FLOWERS

Tropical flowers stand alone beautifully. Ginger, heliconia, and bird of paradise are marvelously sculptural shapes that have strong impact on their own and don't need to be mixed with other flowers to be effective. They tend to be more expensive but you do not need as many stems to make a dramatic arrangement. A few tall or broad tropical leaves work well with these flowers and, in fact, their addition allows you to use even fewer blooms and reduce the cost. Many men who normally do not appreciate flowers that much still respond to the colors and drama offered by tropicals. It is best not to try to mix "fluffy" or garden flowers with tropicals unless you are a more advanced designer. It is very tricky. The possible exception is orchids. Although orchids are "tropical" flowers they work well with both tropical bouquets and traditional ones. Orchids combine quite nicely with roses. They also stand so beautifully on their own that a single stem in a vase is gorgeous.

ADD SOMETHING SURPRISING

Try to include something unusual and unexpected among your flowers or in the vase when you are designing an arrangement. An unusual bloom like a lotus blossom or some unnamed wild flower from

above Bright, hot colors mix well and can generate strong, happy feelings.

your garden can add a wonderful unexpected effect. Unusual elements in a floral arrangement invite closer attention. Exotic leaves, pods, berries, fruit, or even vegetables are a nice touch. Filling your clear vase with shells, rocks, or small fruit like kumquats is a nice but easy touch. A few asparagus or artichokes mixed with your flowers can be totally unexpected and delightful. Line or wrap your container with large leaves or tie your bouquet into a nosegay and drop it into your vase for an interesting change. You can even submerge certain blooms completely in water in a clear vase and amaze your friends with your ingenuity.

ONE FLOWER

There are certain flowers that are naturally so lovely or fascinating—or rare—that they do not need to be mixed with other blooms. Some of these are the ones that have the shortest seasons, like everybody's favorite peonies. Then there is lilac, lily of the valley, calla lilies, or the multitudinous varieties of unusual garden roses. Some flowers like tulips and narcissus are at their most beautiful when gathered together in a mass with nothing added. A bouquet of white

narcissus. An armful of sunflowers. A bundle
of hydrangea. A fistful of violets. In each season
nothing can surpass the beauty of these blooms.
Of course that is not to say that you do not
ever want to include these in a mixed bouquet.
Peonies added to lilac or hydrangea added to
a mixed bouquet of roses and tulips can be
quite breathtaking.

GREEN

Green goes with just about anything although
you do need to pay some attention to the shade
of green you mix with other colors. Green is
a trendy color for flowers now, especially
the hotter more acid shades, so growers are
developing great tones of green flowers such
as Jade and Green Tea roses, green cymbidium
orchids, various shades of green hydrangea, and
deep saturated green trachyllium. A little bit
of acid green can spark many other colors. It
makes pinks, browns, and oranges really come
alive. It adds wonderful depth and dimension to
a mixed arrangement. If you don't have green
flowers, drop a few limes into your vase and it
can serve the same purpose.

above Pinks and pastels can project
feminine and youthful qualities.

opposite page, top left

Tropical flowers are best mixed with other tropicals.

opposite page, top right

Unusual elements like poppy pods and lotus pods add a surprise touch.

opposite page, bottom left

There is nothing more beautiful than a vase of peonies on their own.

opposite page, bottom right

Green flowers and leaves combine naturally with any other color.

SMALL THINGS TO CONSIDER

* If you are intimidated when you look at an empty vase, try gathering the flowers together in your hand and make a nosegay. Tie it together, cut the stems to one length and drop the entire bouquet into a vase.

*Use a vase with a small mouth that holds your flowers close together. It is easier to design than using a wide mouth vase that requires more flowers and allows excessive movement of the stems.

* For larger mouth vases, use florist tape to make a grid across the top of your vase to help hold the flowers upright. Otherwise, twist some curly willow or vines in the bottom of the vase to hold the stems in place.

* Sometimes it is easier and just as effective to make a variety of small vases to be placed around the house or gathered together in a grouping on your dining table. Use containers that are about 5" or 6" tall and not more than 5" wide. It is fun to mix different sizes and shapes. Look through your cupboards to find unusual containers like teapots, creamers, or unusual glasses.

* Think about adding some texture like berries, greenery, or pods to your arrangement. Big flowers like hydrangea not only add texture but fill space and help to hold your other flowers in place.

* To help your flowers last longer, clean your vase with bleach to remove all bacteria and fill it with cold or room temperature water. Floral nutrients can help prolong their life. Cut stems at an angle. Woody stems like lilac are best if hammered and broken at the ends to facilitate absorbing water. Always keep flowers in a cool place, away from heat and out of direct sunshine. Change the water each day.

* When selecting flowers for entertaining buy them early enough to open fully the day of your party but do not buy them too early as they will be past their prime. Do the arrangements a day ahead so you do not need to worry about them on the day.

conversion charts

Weights and measures have been rounded up or down slightly to make measuring easier.

Volume equivalents:

American	Metric	Imperial
1 teaspoon	5 ml	
1 tablespoon	15 ml	
¼ cup	60 ml	2 fl.oz.
⅓ cup	75 ml	2½ fl.oz.
½ cup	125 ml	4 fl.oz.
⅔ cup	150 ml	5 fl.oz. (¼ pint)
¾ cup	175 ml	6 fl.oz.
1 cup	250 ml	8 fl.oz.

Weight equivalents:

Imperial	Metric
1 oz.	25 g
2 oz.	50 g
3 oz.	75 g
4 oz.	125 g
5 oz.	150 g
6 oz.	175 g
7 oz.	200 g
8 oz. (½ lb.)	250 g
9 oz.	275 g
10 oz.	300 g
11 oz.	325 g
12 oz.	375 g
13 oz.	400 g
14 oz.	425 g
15 oz.	475 g
16 oz. (1 lb.)	500 g
2 lb.	1 kg

Measurements:

Inches	Cm
¼ inch	5 mm
½ inch	1 cm
¾ inch	1.5 cm
1 inch	2.5 cm
2 inches	5 cm
3 inches	7 cm
4 inches	10 cm
5 inches	12 cm
6 inches	15 cm
7 inches	18 cm
8 inches	20 cm
9 inches	23 cm
10 inches	25 cm
11 inches	28 cm
12 inches	30 cm

Oven temperatures:

110°C	(225°F)	Gas ¼
120°C	(250°F)	Gas ½
140°C	(275°F)	Gas 1
150°C	(300°F)	Gas 2
160°C	(325°F)	Gas 3
180°C	(350°F)	Gas 4
190°C	(375°F)	Gas 5
200°C	(400°F)	Gas 6
220°C	(425°F)	Gas 7
230°C	(450°F)	Gas 8
240°C	(475°F)	Gas 9

In Appreciation

With special gratitude to Noelle Brown and Florence Brown for their constant encouragement and support and for opening the door to our first book and to Christina Held for keeping us organized and on track, as always. Thank you to Hans Boer for searching the world for our gorgeous flowers, Daniel Dreyer of Hermes, and Danielle Waldman of Stephen Young Co. for helping us obtain many of our beautiful table settings and Loree Valle for loaning us her vintage California pottery. Thank you to our wonderful clients and especially those who generously offered their heartwarming comments for these pages and those who opened their homes to us for photography. And special gratitude to our incredible team of Mark's Garden floral designers who contributed to these parties: Luis "Cesar" Martinez, Vinnie Bui, Marco Calderon, Anselmo "Manny" Cosmes, Greg Delossantos, Jesus Felipe-Frausto, Owen Foster, Shahnaz Hanasab, Abraham Hernandez, Jose "Frankie" Hernandez, Lourdes Holguin, Anna Mayer, Leo Moreno, Christine Scheer, and Cindy Smith

Mark Held and Richard David
of Mark's Garden

Many thanks to my co-authors, Mark Held and Richard David for inviting me to participate in this book. Their glorious flowers and décor are an inspiration for The Kitchen to provide the finest of food and drink. Brent Sherman and Megan Slaughter were of immense help in the shepherding and display of the food for the photo shoots. Brent's drinks taste as delicious as they look and Megan's help with revising our recipes was excellent. Thank you to: Classic Party Rentals and Ken Antonioli, who generously provided the rental equipment which so enhanced the party photos. Jerry Kohl kindly loaned us his handsome glasses from Brighton Inc., for the Moroccan Party. Fran Bigelow, owner of Fran's Chocolates Ltd. for her excellent chocolates and yummy idea for the Chocolate Covered Figs. Mr. Bob Sutcliffe who graciously helped us with many details regarding the book. Our great clients who kindly allowed us to invade their beautiful homes and never complained. The Kitchen staff who did their usual fine job in preparation of the food and to whom I am always indebted. My husband, Taylor Dark and our family for their patience and love over these many years.

Peggy Dark
of The Kitchen